ART PARKS

A Tour of America's Sculpture Parks and Gardens

ART PARKS

A Tour of America's Sculpture Parks and Gardens

Francesca Cigola

Princeton Architectural Press
New York

WEST   MIDWEST

SOUTH/SOUTHWEST   **NORTHEAST**

CONTENTS

Catherine Seavitt Nordenson

PREFACE

Historically, sculpture in the American park consisted primarily of memorial statuary, figural monuments on thick bases that connected a particular place to past events. But a transformative shift began in the late nineteenth century. Consider New York's Central Park. Frederick Law Olmsted and Calvert Vaux did include statuary as part of its original Greensward Plan; they defined the formal allée of elm trees that line the Mall as a "Literary Walk" with statues of authors and poets, including Shakespeare and Sir Walter Scott. However, Olmsted and Vaux were wary of the intrusion of sculpture into the park—the accumulation of these "details and accessories," they argued, would diminish the intended pictorial effects of the long natural vistas. They saw the park itself as a work of art, its landscape both foreground and background. It was not to serve as a backdrop to monumental sculpture.[1]

As Rosalind Krauss notes in her influential essay of 1979 "Sculpture in the Expanded Field," this shift transformed sculpture: it became nomadic, uprooted from any connection to a site. Referring to two of Auguste Rodin's sculptures, Monument to Balzac and The Gates of Hell, Krauss writes: "With these two sculptural projects, I would say, one crosses the threshold of the logic of the monument, entering the space of what could be called its negative condition—a kind of sitelessness, or homelessness, an absolute loss of place. Which is to say one enters modernism."[2] Krauss then uses Klein-group logic to diagram the new network of relationships that sculpture might inhabit in the postmodern period; the artist could now occupy and invent various positions in an expanded field including landscape and architecture: "site construction," "marked sites," "axiomatic structures," "sculpture." Artists were the inventors of new relationships between art and the park.

For Krauss, the artist Robert Smithson represented this new breed of sculptor, the land artist. Seeking a dialectical relationship between art and place, Smithson considered Olmsted's Central Park an ideal model—its sculpture was embedded in its geologic terrain. He saw the art of sculpture in the park's Vista Rock tunnel along the Seventy-Ninth Street transverse road, where live rock was carved into both form and infrastructure. Water seeps mysteriously from the tunnel's rock crevices, forming icicles in the winter. For Smithson, Olmsted was the first "earthwork artist." Central Park was an incomplete thing, operating in a temporal continuum of natural processes. "Olmsted's parks exist before they are finished, which means in fact they are never finished; they remain carriers of the unexpected and of contradiction on all levels of human activity, be it social, political, or natural."[3]

When we visit and view the fantastic catalogue of American art parks presented by Francesca Cigola in this volume, it is wonderful to contemplate both the works of sculpture themselves and the very parks in which they are embedded, forever slipping into foreground, background, time, and perception.

1 Frederick Law Olmsted, "The Proper Function of Statuary in the Park," in Central Park as a Work of Art and as a Great Municipal Enterprise, ed. Frederick Law Olmsted Jr. and Theodora Kimball (New York: G. P. Putnam's Sons, 1928), 486–98.
2 Rosalind Krauss, "Sculpture in the Expanded Field," October 8 (1979): 34.
3 Robert Smithson, "Frederick Law Olmsted and the Dialectical Landscape," Artforum, February 1973, 62.

13

INTRODUCTION

The American landscape has been depicted from a multitude of perspectives, each attributing to it a distinctive identity, role, or aesthetic. This landscape has been seen at different times as a supplier of natural resources, a territory to be conquered, a subject for scientific study, a symbol of national identity, a series of ecosystems to be safeguarded, a focus of environmental activism, or simply as a place for leisure activities.

In recent decades, it has become increasingly popular to use the landscape for another purpose: as outdoor art space. Such spaces (known variously as art parks, sculpture parks, sculpture gardens, or outdoor art collections) are growing in number due to an increasing tendency to view the land through an aesthetic lens. Works of art in these spaces interact with surrounding landscapes, playing off of their character, colors, and makeup; in many cases the boundaries between the works and their settings are blurred.

The concept of the art park, loosely defined as an open space where the landscape and works of art are designed and arranged to coexist, dates all the way back to the Renaissance and can be traced to both public and private spaces in urban and rural settings throughout Europe.

In the United States, avant-garde artists have used art and landscape since the 1960s as tools of liberation capable of breaking down the barriers erected by more traditional methods for displaying public art. They have introduced new methods for interpreting and manipulating places through art, in natural environments (where large-scale land art has been created in remote, less populated areas), urban settings that feature public art (perhaps best symbolized by Eero Saarinen's *Gateway Arch* in St. Louis, Missouri) or on the grounds of institutions that have seen these changes and adapted them for their own use.

At the same time, new techniques for industrially producing massive sculptures launched a new outdoor art tradition—still active today—of works that match the large scale of North America's wide-open spaces.

Although land art is not yet prominent in sculpture parks, some parks have introduced increasing numbers of site-specific or ephemeral works with an eye to related principles such as sustainability. As John K. Grande writes in his essay "The Ephemeral Sculpture Garden" (in *Landscapes for Art: Contemporary Sculpture Parks*, ISC Press), "new ephemeral sculpture has transformed Land Art into eco-art, no longer necessarily large scale, but sensitive to biology and geology, and even to more transparent and transient effects like climate."

The meaning and the environmental matrix of site-specific works make them a type of art that is particularly well suited to the mission of art parks, echoing the teachings and goals of environmental artists and their work on reclaiming and regenerating abused landscapes. The art park, in its various forms, sizes, and meanings, can generally be defined as a place where landscape and works of art are conceived and often planned to play off of each other. In some cases (the Minneapolis Sculpture Garden at the Walker Art Center is an excellent example), the landscape takes the form of a true outdoor gallery, a series of rooms constructed out of plant materials.

Art parks and gardens are found in both urban and rural settings throughout North America. They take many different forms and have been created in all sorts of ways. As a result, their makeup, the terminology used to describe them, and the degree to which they interact with their surrounding spaces varies widely. Indeed, so many of these parks have been created in recent decades and they differ so much from each other that it's hard to develop any hard-and-fast rules for categorizing them. They can, however, be grouped loosely by certain general characteristics, and these groupings can in turn inform an understanding of how this phenomenon has evolved in a land as vast and varied as North America.

The parks that follow have been organized into three categories: leisure spaces, learning spaces, and collectors' spaces. This book is meant to serve as a guide, identifying the distinctive characteristics of the parks and the ways in which they can be enjoyed.

Leisure spaces are natural or urban parks (the smallest and most intimate are sculpture gardens) where visitors walk among natural elements and the works themselves, taking what can truly be called an art and nature walk. The Storm King Art Center, located in New York's Hudson Valley and one of the first such spaces, dates back to the 1960s and revolves around a collection that has expanded to cover almost five hundred acres. Such sculpture parks are usually located outside of cities and created to serve as homes for works of art that are either acquired or created on site and that interact with and complement the surrounding natural environment.

Often such parks are works in progress, where new temporary or permanent works of various types are added or sometimes even specifically commissioned. Many of them contain land art and environmental art. Good examples are Olympic Sculpture Park in Seattle, Millennium Park in Chicago, and *California Scenario* in Costa Mesa. They interact with their respective cities and play off of their skylines, which become part of the parks' open-air settings.

Even before large-scale sculpture came into vogue in the 1960s, many museums and university art collections had begun to commission such works in open spaces in and around their buildings, where art could be viewed in an open-air setting. Perhaps the best-known example of this resides within the Museum of Modern Art in New York City. The earliest designs for the building included space for a sculpture garden, and today the museum houses the Abby Aldrich Rockefeller Sculpture Garden. Such learning spaces within museums and universities have an educational purpose. They are intended to encourage the contemplation of sculpture in open-air galleries, using a model that has come to be called a museum without walls or open-air museum. The scale, urban character, and architectural nature of these spaces make them true sculpture gardens that function as individual parts of larger institutions. Some, like the Hirshhorn Museum and Sculpture Garden, even share equal billing with the host institution.

These large-scale art parks and museum sculpture gardens are open to the public and offer visitors a chance to experience and learn about art. A third type of park, the collectors' space, is more likely to house a private collection. These typically originated as impressive outdoor displays surrounding the homes of collectors and artists. They are often intimate and highly personal, due to their associations with house-museums or studio-museums; often the original layouts and locations of the pieces are maintained. Counted among them are the Noguchi Museum, designed by Isamu Noguchi himself, and the Chinati Foundation, created by Donald Judd in Marfa, Texas, as well as Kykuit, the Rockefeller residence in Tarrytown, New York; Kentuck Knob in Chalk Hill, Pennsylvania, the property of Lady and Lord Palumbo; or the Oliver Ranch Foundation in Geyserville, California.

Christine Tarkowski, **Working on the Failed Utopia,** 2005

In addition, during the postwar era, corporate campuses began to appear in the United States, generally in areas outside of cities that offered enough open space to house both large manufacturing facilities and office space. These campuses are usually found in idyllic, pastoral landscapes that offer sharp contrast to the industrial character of the workplace. Their large-scale architecture brings the man-made to natural areas. With an eye to the physical and psychological well-being of workers, many companies have endowed these campuses with art parks. Green space with common areas and sometimes even artificial lakes transform these campuses from mere workplaces into small cities in their own right.

An art park is a hybrid: a merger of art and landscape, a "landscape structure" designed to house large works. Art parks are designed to welcome the public, as a place where the viewer is invited to experience the work (both art and landscape) on multiple levels of perception and interaction.

LEISURE SPACES

(top) Margaret Evangeline, **Gunshot Landscape**, 2004; (bottom) Oliver Kruse, **Clench**, 2008

The Fields Sculpture Park

Omi International Arts Center, Omi, New York

Omi International Arts Center is a not-for-profit organization that runs residency programs for artists. The related Fields Sculpture Park sits on more than sixty acres
of green space. Part of the park hosts large-scale site-specific works by contemporary
American and international artists.

The park was founded in 1998 by Francis Greenburger, who wanted to offer a
space that would be open to the public and could house innovative works that would
be integrated into the natural environment. That environment is divided into nine different areas; more than seventy pieces have been installed over the years, and a thematic
show is staged every June that includes new works. The shows' themes are related to
the relationships among art, nature, and landscape. The Ignoring Boundaries series
has included *Image in the Landscape* (Part 1–2001); *Sound in the Landscape* (Part
2–2002); *Into the Gloaming* (Part 3–2003); *Public Notice: Painting in the Landscape*
(Part 4–2004); *Nature/Not Nature* (2007); and *Into the Trees* (2008, title drawn from
the Ernest Hemingway story "Across the River and Into the Trees"), in which nine artists were invited to create site-specific works using the park's trees as a jumping-off
point. Well-known artists such as Bernar Venet (2002), Charles Ginnever (2003), and
Tom Gottsleben (2005) have held solo shows in the park. In 2011, Alice Aycock's *A
Simple Network of Underground Wells and Tunnels* was constructed under the artist's supervision; this work had originally been installed in New Jersey in 1975 and has
had extraordinary impact on both land art and architecture. The Charles B. Benenson
Visitors Center and Gallery, which stands at the entry to the park and includes a cafe,
is used for exhibits and events. Named for a major supporter of the center, it was built
in strict compliance with the latest guidelines for environmental sustainability.

Roy Staab, **Green Galleon**, 2008

THE FIELDS SCULPTURE PARK Omi International Arts Center, 405 County Route 22, Ghent, NY 12075
INFO (518) 392-4747; www.artomi.org   **ARTISTS** Magdalena Abakanowicz, MM Anderson, Carl Andre, Barbara
Andrus, William Anastasi, Alice Aycock, Lillian Ball, Ulrich Bauss, Jane Benson, Willard Boepple, Philip Boehn,
Stanley Boxer, Dove Bradshaw, Steven Brower, Fritz Buehner, Joyce Burstein, Alexander Calder, Mary Ellen Carroll,
Michael Cataldi, Jed Cleary, Tony Cragg, James Croak, John Cross, Tarik Currimbhoy, Lewis DeSoto, Dan Devine,
Peter Dudek, Mikala Dwyer, Nancy Dwyer, Janet Echelman, Olafur Eliasson, Margaret Evangeline, Lauren Ewing,
Miloslav Fekar, Jackie Ferrara, Linda Fleming, David Frank, Kathleen Gilrain, Charles Ginnever, Dewitt Godfrey,
Ronald Gonzalez, Harry Gordon, Tom Gottlesben, Philip Grausman, Robert Grosvenor, Tadashi Hashimoto, Peter
Hide, Jene Highstein, J. Shih Chieh Huang, John Isherwood, Jae-Choul Jeoung, Kahn|Selesnick, Baris Karayazgan,
Nina Katchadourian, Habib Kheradyar, Alain Kirili, Grace Knowlton, Oliver Kruse, Ann Jon, Ken Laudauer, Nina Levy,
Alexander Liberman, Donald Lipski, Robert Lobe, Mary Mattingly, Thomas Matsuda, Vincent Mazeau, John Powers,
Antoni Milkowski, Forrest Myers, Stefanie Nagorka, Richard Nonas, Nova Mihai Popa, Erin O'Keefe, Don Osborn,
Shimon Okshteyn, Dennis Oppenheim, Alena Ort, Don Osborn, Victoria Palermo, Beverly Pepper, Robert Perless,
Joanna Przybyla, Gary Quinonez, Steven Rand, Dina Recanati, Michael Rees, Erwin Redi, Brian Ripel, Steven Rolf
Kroeger, Mia Westerlund Roosen, Tony Rosenthal, John Ruppert, Tim Scott, Foon Sham, Hyungsub Shin, Jean Shin,
Lisa Solomon, Michael Somoroff, Roy Staab, Peter Stempel, Jeff Talman, Type A, William Tucker, Mary Ann Unger,
Xavier Veilhan, Bernar Venet, Ole Videbaek, Bill Wilson, Isaac Witkin   **SCULPTURES 73**

Charles Ginnever, **Apollo**, 1985

Bernar Venet, **5 Arcs × 5**, 2000

Larry W. Griffis Jr., **Rohr Hill Sculptures**, ca. 1966

Griffis Sculpture Park

East Otto, New York

Griffis Sculpture Park was created as with the intention of combining art and nature. When it opened in 1966, it was one of the first completely open parks in the United States. It was founded by Larry W. Griffis Jr., who had been charmed by Hadrian's Villa in Tivoli during a trip to Italy. He searched long and hard and finally found a piece of land in Ashford Hollow where he could install some of his work. The Ashford Hollow Foundation for the Visual and Performing Arts was founded to manage the park; it is currently headed by Damian Griffis.

Over the years, the size of the park has grown (thanks to the later acquisition of adjacent land), and the number of works has grown as well. There are currently two hundred pieces in the park, donated by the artists.

The landscape in this park is extremely varied. There are approximately 445 acres of land, which allow visitors to be immersed completely in a natural setting and to interact fully with the installed sculptures. One thing that differentiates this park from most other art parks is the extent of interaction among art, nature, and audience: visitors are encouraged not only to look at the art, but to interact with it as if it were a natural element. In other words, they are welcome to touch the sculptures, walk through them, and even climb them. The installations are both figurative and abstract and are broken down into twelve thematic groups. Pieces include architectural compositions (*Wood Pallet Egg* is an ovoid structure made of pallets assembled and created by the architects Mehrdad Hadighi and Frank Fantauzzi); large-scale anthropomorphic structures; insects; and surreal, primitive figures.

Frank Fantauzzi, Mehrdad Hadighi, **Wood Pallet Egg**, 2010

GRIFFIS SCULPTURE PARK 6902 Mill Valley Road, East Otto, NY 14729
INFO (716) 667-2808; www.griffispark.org **ARTISTS** Joe Bolinski, Dwain, Frank Fantauzzi, Larry W. Griffis Jr., Mark Griffis, Mehrdad Hadighi, Duayne Hatchett, Tony Paterson, Glenn Zweygardt **SCULPTURES** 250

(top) Steven Siegel, **Facing love; 30**, 1999; (bottom) John von Bergen, **Grande Comore II**, 2004

Stone Quarry Hill Art Park

Cazenovia, New York

Founded by Dorothy and Robert Riester and open to the public since 1991, Stone Quarry Hill is a nature preserve of approximately one hundred acres in central New York State.

Paths crisscross the park and weave through the landscape. Numerous natural sculptures and installations dot the lawns, woods, and vistas, offering a dual experience of immersion in both art and nature.

Many of the artists whose sculptures are displayed here work with natural elements. These include Patrick Dougherty with one of his stickworks, *Off the Beaten Path* (2002); Steven Siegel with his work made of newspapers and branches found on site; and Sook Jin Jo, a Korean artist who lives in New York, with her *Meditation Space* (2000), an organic geometric form made of tree trunks that compose a natural room from which the surrounding countryside can be admired.

The park remains open in the winter and offers sports facilities. It also runs a residence program for artists; participants take part in an annual exhibit, and their works are then added to the park's permanent collection.

Sook Jin Jo, **Meditation Space**, 2000

STONE QUARRY HILL ART PARK 3883 Stone Quarry Road, Cazenovia, NY 13035
INFO (315) 655-3196; www.stonequarryhillartpark.org   **ARTISTS** Barbara Andrus, Reiko Aoyagi, Diane Banks, Emilie Benes Brzezinski, Michele Brody, Patrick Dougherty, John Fitzsimmons, Joan Giroux, Frank Gonzales, Rita Hammond, Cindi Harper, David Harper, Fritz Horstman, Sook Jin Jo, Jonathan Kirk, Eva Lapka, Denise Stillwaggon Leone, Dariusz Lipski, Enriquo Lopez-Chicheri, Rodger Mack, John McCarty, Ene Osteraas, Dorothy Riester, Steven Siegel, Takashi Soga, Gligor Stefanov, John Von Bergen, Pat Warner, Matt Weber, Susan Winks, Al Zaruba   **SCULPTURES** approximately 70

Maya Lin, **Storm King Wave Field**, 2009

STORM KING ART CENTER 1 Museum Road, New Windsor, NY 12553   **INFO** (845) 534-3115; www.stormking.org
ARTISTS Magdalena Abakanowicz, Douglas Abdell, Phoebe Adams, Kosta Alex, Carl Andre, Oliver Andrews, David
Annesley, Siah Armajani, Boris Aronson, Alice Aycock, Saul Baizerman, Lynda Benglis, Harry Bertoia, Max Bill, Klaus
Blackmund, Ronald Bladen, Helaine Blumefeld, Willard Boepple, Chakaia Booker, Louise Bourgeois, Manuel Bromberg,
Thom Brown, Daniel Buren, Pol Bury, Alexander Calder, Kenneth Campbell, Kenneth Capps, Anthony Caro, Victor
Contreras, George Cutts, Dorothy Dehner, Tony DeLap, Louis Derbe, Mark di Suvero, Jean Dubuffet, John Duff, Ludvik
Durchanek, Kosso Eloul, Henri Etienne-Martin, Sorel Etrog, Herbert Ferber, Nino Franchina, Mary Frank, Richard
Friedberg, Sue Fuller, Roland Gebhardt, Arthur Gibbons, Charles Ginnever, Andy Goldsworthy, Elizabeth Gordon,
Adolph Gottlieb, Emilio Greco, Robert Grosvenor, Bruno Groth, Raoul Hague, Thomas Hardy, Gilbert Hawkins, Milton
Hebald, Barbara Hepworth, Elijah David Herschler, Isabella Howland, Hans Hokanson, Alfred Hrdlicka, Richard Hunt,
Jim Huntington, Patricia Johanson, Donald Judd, Eli Karpel, Menashe Kadishman, Mel Kendrick, Sybil Kennedy, Lyman
Kipp, Jerome Kirk, John Knight, Grace Knowlton, Fritz Koenig, Joseph Konzal, Joseph Kurhajec, Yayoi Kusama, Dennis
Leon, Sol Lewitt, Alexander Liberman, Roy Lichtenstein, Maya Lin, Robert Lobe, Hubert Long, Giacomo Manzu, Dorothy
Mayhall , Ethel Meyers, Tomio Miki, Luciano Minguzzi, Henry Moore, Robert Murray, Forrest Myers, Mario Negri, Louise
Nevelson, John Newman, Isamu Noguchi, Ann Norton, Anthony Padovano, Nam June Paik, Eduardo Paolozzi, Louis
Pearson, Beverly Pepper, Humberto Peraza, Joel Perlman, Karl Pfann, Josef Pillhofer, Arnaldo Pomodoro, Stephen
Porter, Leo Rabkin, Peter Reginato, Reinhoud, George Rickey, Risa, Mia Westerlund Roosen, Lucas Samaras, Hans
Schleeh, Melvin Schuler, Tim Scott, Richard Serra, Yehiel Shemi, Richard Shore, Charles Simonds, Yerassimos
Sklavos, David Smith, Kenneth Snelson, Ann Sperry, Richard Stankiewicz, Michael Steiner, Jan Peter Stern, David
Stoltz, Tal Streeter, George Sugarman, Johnny Swing, Erwin Thorn, Michael Todd, Tomonori Toyofuka, Lee Tribe, Ernest
Trova, William Tucker, Veronica van Eyck, Ursula von Rydingsvard, David von Schlegell, Frieda Vredaparis, Theodore
Waddell, Gerald Walburg, Paul Waldman, Elbert Weinberg, Alice Winant, Isaac Witkin, James Wolfe, Fritz Wortruba,
Ossip Zadkine   **SCULPTURES** 120   **LANDSCAPE DESIGN** William A. Rutherford   **REFERENCES** Stern, H. Peter, and Peter
A. Bienstock. *Earth, Sky and Sculpture: Storm King Art Center.* Mountainville, NY: Storm King Art Center, 2009.

Storm King Art Center

Mountainville, New York

Storm King Art Center sits on close to five hundred acres of meadows and wooded areas in the Hudson Valley and houses more than 120 sculptures by internationally renowned artists. The park was created by Ralph E. Ogden and H. Peter Stern in 1960, and new sculptures have been added over the years. This eventually led to the idea of integrating the art into the surrounding countryside, which was designed by landscape architect William A. Rutherford.

Initially, the park had been conceived as a gallery for local artists from the Hudson River School, but the founders grew increasingly interested in sculpture, which led to an early acquisition of thirteen works by David Smith (1906–1965). These are grouped on a hill created for this purpose and interact with each other, just as the artist had conceived them and had installed them in his own studio-park in Bolton Landing, New York.

In 1972 Storm King began to collect largely abstract works by both American and European artists, either as part of its permanent collection or as long-term loans from other institutions. Four of Alexander Calder's stabiles are on permanent loan from the Calder Foundation of New York; these date to the later period of the artist's life, from 1974 to 1976, and they sit on the eastern hill of the park. They are in Calder's typically lively colors. Calder's sinuous and monumental *Arch* (1975, acquired in 1982) welcomes visitors at the entrance to the center.

After Ogden's death in 1974, Stern continued to add to the art in the park and develop it further. In 1977 Isamu Noguchi was commissioned to make *Momotaro,* considered one of his most sophisticated works. This monumental and poetic stone sculpture, dedicated to a traditional Japanese folk hero born from a peach pit, is one of the few interactive works in this location. Another interactive sculpture is *Gazebo for Two Anarchists: Gabriella Antolini and Alberto Antolini* (1992) by Iranian artist Siah Armajani. Mark di Suvero's impressive sculptures (*Mahatma,* 1978–79; *Mon Père, Mon Père,* 1973–75; *Mother Peace,* 1969–70; and *Pyramidian,* 1987–98) mark off a planted area at the foot of the main hill at regular intervals, creating a single collective work that takes the form of an elegant series of steel structures. Richard Serra was also invited to create a site-specific work, and he chose to locate it at the park's border: *Schunnemunk Fork* (1991) is a group of four monumental steel plates partially buried in the ground that draw the visitor's gaze to the surrounding area. Another site-specific work is Andy Goldsworthy's *Storm King Wall* (1997–98). This piece is built of stones collected on site and winds toward the trees until it dips into a nearby pond, then comes out on the other side and continues on its way.

The variety of works, the unexpected scale of the sculptures in relation to the land, and the surprising beauty of the countryside make Storm King one of the country's most elegant sculpture parks. In addition to the works acquired and commissioned over the years, others have been added to the collection from the temporary exhibits that are held annually, such as *For Paul* (1990–92/2001) by Ursula von Rydingsvard, created during three periods over the course of ten years following its first exhibit at Storm King. Other works have been donated by the artists themselves, such as Magdalena Abakanowicz's *Sarcophagi in Glass Houses* (1989, donated in 1994) and Alice Aycock's *Three-Fold Manifestation* (donated in 1987, refurbished in 2006), inspired by the upward motion of influences as wide-ranging as Constantin Brancusi's sculptures, Leonardo da Vinci's drawings, and Walter Gropius's designs.

The park's most recent site-specific work was installed in spring 2009: *Storm King Wave Field* by artist and architect Maya Lin is a series of undulating masses made of earth designed to simulate water in motion. The 2012 exhibit *Light and Landscape* explored the work of fourteen artists who use light as an artistic medium.

Mark di Suvero, **Pyramidian**, 1987/98 (left, background); **Mon Père, Mon Père**, 1973–75 (center); and **Mother Peace**, 1969–70 (right)

Alissa Neglia, **Lace** (from the exhibition *Escape Velocity*), 1998

Socrates Sculpture Park

Long Island City, New York

Socrates Sculpture Park is an experimental, alternative park. At the time of its creation in Queens, on the banks of the East River, it was seen as a utopian effort and a pioneer in the neighborhood. A coalition of artists developed the park as an autonomous space intended to be used for the on-site production of the works to be exhibited. Over the last twenty years, it has been utterly transformed. The former industrial site has been cleaned up and now serves as a gathering place and event space for the local community and, above all, according to Thomas Hanrahan in his essay "Urban Space as Work of Art" (in *Socrates Sculpture Park,* Yale University Press), a "new urban space dedicated to learning and artistic production, one that [is] egalitarian in spirit and open to everyone regardless of class, education or race."

Mark di Suvero, who founded the park in 1986—naming it in honor of Socrates and his lifelong search for truth—saw the potential for this piece of abandoned land along the East River and supported its development through his Athena Foundation. Today the park, revitalized and redesigned over the years, serves as a meeting place for young artists, visitors to this small but significant arts district (the Noguchi Museum, MoMA PS1, and SculptureCenter are all nearby), and neighborhood residents, who use the open space freely. The park has had more than sixty-five thousand visitors since it opened, many of them attending events, which attract large audiences. More than five hundred artists have worked in the outdoor space, and more than fifty exhibits have been organized there to display large-scale works, transforming the very space itself into a work of art. The artists who have exhibited at Socrates Sculpture Park include Mark di Suvero, Charles Ginnever, Keith Haring, Tom Otterness, David Shapiro, Bernar Venet, George Segal, and Magdalena Abakanowicz.

Lishan Chang, **LC Space @ SSP** (from the exhibition *Float*), 2007

SOCRATES SCULPTURE PARK 32-01 Vernon Boulevard, Long Island City, NY 11106
INFO (718) 956-1819; www.socratessculpturepark.org ROTATING EXHIBITS
REFERENCES Baker, Alyson, Ivana Mestrovic, and Robyn Donohue. *Socrates Sculpture Park.* New Haven, CT: Yale University Press, 2006.

(top) Isaac Witkin, **Eolith**, 1994; (bottom) Carlos Dorrien, **The Nine Muses**, 1990–97

Grounds for Sculpture

Hamilton, New Jersey

This park, which opened in 1992, is located about twenty minutes from the Princeton University campus on a former fairgrounds site. Grounds for Sculpture sits on a property of about thirty-five acres, encompassing house galleries, gardens, and courtyards, all of which are dotted with two hundred or so contemporary sculptures. The large-scale abstract and figurative pieces come mostly from museum collections; some are on temporary loan. Founded by J. Seward Johnson Jr., a sculptor and philanthropist, for the purpose of making sculpture accessible to as many people as possible, the park is now run by a nonprofit public organization and offers a variety of experiences and ways to commune with nature, from viewing the outdoor sculptures to visiting the arboretum. A wide array of different areas for leisure activities and relaxation, as well indoor exhibit spaces, can be found in this purposefully informal setting that is markedly different from the more rigid atmosphere of a traditional museum.

In just a few years, the collection has expanded to include works by internationally renowned artists including Clement Meadmore, Anthony Caro, Beverly Pepper, Kiki Smith, George Segal, and Alexander Liberman. Today it is the most significant outdoor museum in New Jersey. Some of the works were commissioned for the park, such as *Space of Stone* by Magdalena Abakanowicz, one of her largest installations, and *Garden State* by Isaac Witkin. The park also organizes temporary solo shows and has an artists' residency program. In 2004 the resident was Patrick Dougherty, and for four weeks he invited volunteers of all ages to participate in the construction of one of his signature ephemeral installations.

GROUNDS FOR SCULPTURE 18 Fairgrounds Road, Hamilton, NJ 08619 **INFO** (609) 586-0616; www.groundsforsculpture.org **ARTISTS** Magdalena Abakanowicz, Lalitha Anantharaman, Bill Barrett, James Barton, Bruce Beasley, Tova Beck-Friedman, Raffael Benazzi, Emilie Benes Brzezinski, Itzik Benshalom, Fletcher Benton, Curt Brill, Benbow Bullock, Christopher Cairns, Anthony Caro, Lynden Cline, James Colavita, Susan Crowder, Robert Cooke, Linda Cunningham, Joan Danziger, David E. Davis, David Allen Devrishian, James Dinerstein, Michele Oka Doner, William Donnan, Carlos Dorrien, Patrick Dougherty, Walter Dusenbery, Horace Farlowe, Carole A. Feuerman, Leonda Finke, Rob Fisher, Béla Fűkő, Charles Ginnever, Daniel Goode, Philip Grausman, Bradford Graves, Red Grooms, Mike Gyampo, Brower Hatcher, Sarah Haviland, Richard Heinrich, Marion Held, John Henry, Gyuri Hollosy, David L. Hostetler, Petro Hul, Jim Huntington, Seymour Ikenson, Jon Isherwood, Luis Jimenez, J. Seward Johnson Jr., Daniel Kainz, Lila Katzen, Mel Kendrick, Niki Ketchman, William King, Stephen Knapp, Berj Krikorian, Jon Lash, Francisco Leiro, Nina Levy, Alexander Liberman, Bruce Lindsay, Sharon Loper, Helena Lukásová, Peter Lundberg, Kevin Lyles, Robert Mangold, Marisol, Jeffrey Maron, John Martini, Patriciu Mateescu, Scott McMillin, Clement Meadmore, Zoran Mojsilov, G. Frederick Morante, Paul Muick, Pat Musick, John Newman, Linda Ogden, Samuel R. Ogden Jr., Mary Oros, Tom Otterness, Barry Parker, Kenneth Payne, Marsha Pels, Beverly Pepper, Joel Perlman, Karen Petersen, Martha Pettigrew, Robert Pfitzenmeier, Don Porcaro, Toni Putnam, Robert Ressler, Andrew Rogers, James Rosati, Dorothy Ruddick, John Ruppert, Alexander Rutsch, Jill Sablosky, George Segal, Mary Shaffer, Ernest Shaw, Steven Siegel, Christoph Spath, Kiki Smith, Larry Steele, Tom Sternal, Dana Stewart, Harmut Stielow, Strong-Cuevas, Patrick Strzelec, George Sugarman, Toshiko Takaezu, Meryl Taradash, Katrina Tatarovich, Gunnar Theel, Wayne Trapp, Hans Van de Bovenkamp, Herk Van Tongeren, Viktor, Stefan Vladescu, Peter Voulkos, Clifford Ward, Gary Wertheim, Jay Wholley, Roy Wilson, Isaac Witkin, Peter Woytuk, Autin Wright, Yuyu Yang, Larry Young, Ron Young, Hyung Jun Yum, Rhea Zinman, Glenn Zweygardt **SCULPTURES** 250

Steven Siegel, **Grass, Paper, Glass**, 2006

(top) Nils-Udo, **Clemson Clay Nest**, Clay, Pinetrees, Bamboos, 2005. Lifochrome on dibond 87 × 100 cm ed.8; (bottom) Herb Parker, **Crucible**, 1995 (rebuilt in 2004)

Nature-Based Sculpture Program

South Carolina Botanical Garden, Clemson, South Carolina

The Nature-Based Sculpture Program at the South Carolina Botanical Garden is run by the botanical garden's cultural division in conjunction with the landscape architecture program at Clemson University.

Each year, artists from around the world are invited to spend one month creating on-site sculptures, assisted by a staff of volunteers and students. These ephemeral works, created with natural materials, are intended to be temporary installations that eventually erode and combine with the surrounding natural environment. They can be viewed during all phases and, depending on the materials used, they have life cycles of fifteen to twenty years.

Each artist is asked to choose an area for his or her work, and each work is intended solely for the chosen site. Artists then work only with natural and living plant materials to create sacred spaces for interacting and connecting with nature. During the residency, each artist holds a series of lectures, and students at Clemson University can participate in the work's construction.

The resulting pieces are located on approximately three hundred acres of parkland. Viewers can explore the natural environment at their own pace rather than following preset routes or using a map. The community is heavily involved; one of the park's main goals is to educate people and impress upon them the importance of environmental friendliness.

The garden's first sculpture, *Crucible,* was created by Herb Parker in 1995 in honor of the natural spring that feeds the stream running next to the park. This is one of the garden's best-known works and was rebuilt in 2004. Patrick Dougherty created his *Sittin' Pretty* in 1996 and *Spittin' Image* in 2004. Alfio Bonanno was in residence in 1997 and created *Natural Dialogue* using a variety of natural elements, including stones, branches, light, and water. *The Stream Path* (1998) by Gilles Bruni and Marc Babarit, built in the riverbed of a small stream almost as if to mark its path through the wooded area of the park, is now almost completely back to its original form, while *The Space in Between* (2000) by Trudi Entwistle, a series of elliptical mounds of earth covered in moss, is still recognizable. Other works that are still visible in the park include *Time Capsule* by Chris Drury (2002); *Earthen Bridge* (1996) by Brian Rust; *Invisible Operations* (1999) by Karen McCoy; *Impressions of Lost Life* (2000) by Kathleen Gilrain; *Ochun* (2000) by Martha Jackson-Jarvis; *The Devotion of the Sunflower* (2003) by Yolanda Gutiérrez; *Clemson Clay Nest* (2005; no longer visible but to be reinstalled) by Nils-Udo; and *A Chameleon Meadow—In Praise of Shadows* (2007) by Yvette Dede and Hiroko Inoue.

Brian Rust, **Earthen Bridge**, 1996 (rebuilt in 2006)

NATURE-BASED SCULPTURE PROGRAM South Carolina Botanical Garden, 150 Discovery Lane, Clemson, SC 29634 **INFO** (864) 656-3405; www.clemson.edu public/scbg/ **ARTISTS** Marc Babarit, Alfio Bonanno, Gilles Bruni, Yvette Dede and Hiroko Inoue, Patrick Dougherty, Chris Drury, Trudi Entwistle, Kathleen Gilrain, Yolanda Gutiérrez, Martha Jackson-Jarvis, Karen McCoy, Nils-Udo, Herb Parker, Brian Rust **SCULPTURES** 12

Lin Emery, **Duo**, 1992

OUTDOOR COLLECTION AND SCULPTURE GARDEN Museum of Outdoor Arts, 1000 Englewood Parkway, Englewood, CO 80110
INFO (303) 806-0444; www.moaonline.org   **ARTISTS** John Adduci, Giovanni Antoniazzi, Barbara Baer, Ken Bortolazzo, Carolyn
Braaksma, Beniamino Bufano, George Carlson, Guy Dill, Patrick Dougherty, Chris Drury, Lin Emery, Red Grooms, Lonnie Hanzon,
Susan Hart, John Hock, Stephen Hokanson, John Isherwood, Marcel Kalberer, Torval Keller, Grace Knowlton, Amy Laugesen,
Jon Leitner, Dennis Leon, George Lundeen, Robert Mangold, Harry Marinsky, Andy Miller, Alissa Neglia, Agnes Nyanhongo, Tony
Ortega, Patty Ortiz, Daniel Ostermiller, Arnaldo Pomodoro, George Rickey, Todd Siler, Kristine Smock, Sanfte Strukturen, Leslie
Alcott Temple, Lynn Tillery, Steve J. Urry, Mark Warwick, Madeline Wiener **SCULPTURES** 150

Outdoor Collection and Sculpture Garden

Museum of Outdoor Arts, Englewood, Colorado

The Museum of Outdoor Arts (MOA) is an open-air art museum focused on the theme of merging urban space, architecture, sculpture, and landscape; it received an American Institute of Architects award for its environmental concept.

Founded in 1981 by John W. Madden Jr. and his daughter Cynthia Madden Leitner, the museum is intended to make art a part of daily life by locating large-size sculptures in specific places in the city. It is located in Englewood, part of the Denver metropolitan area. Started with a collection of nineteen works, the open-air museum now houses more than two hundred in various areas of the city designated by Madden, including closed spaces such as Greenwood Plaza, a classic plaza that was the original focal point of the collection, and the Sculpture Garden, which houses nine contemporary American works acquired from the Sculpture Center of New Jersey. Samson Park (with the adjacent Fiddler's Green Amphitheatre), on a plateau south of Denver facing the Front Range of the Rocky Mountains, houses the largest selection of the works. In addition to sculptures from the *Alice in Wonderland* series (1994) by Harry Marinsky, site-specific works were commissioned. Patrick Dougherty took a month to create an on-site stickwork—a temporary sculpture that incorporates elements from the surrounding vegetation. In 2010 Sanfte Strukturen (the German workshop of Marcel Kalberer, whose botanical sculptures are found in major natural art parks) installed *Weidenblume* (*Willow Flower*), a plant sculpture of willow branches. The artist's first work in the United States, it was created in three weeks and donated by the MOA to Denver's Biennial of the Americas.

In 2000 the MOA opened a location in the Englewood Civic Center, adding to its outdoor collection and installing sculptures in strategic points around the city. Included are kinetic works like George Rickey's *Two Open Trapezoids: Excentric V* (1978) and Lin Emery's *Duo* (2002).

Sanfte Strukturen / Marcel Kalberer, **Weidenblume**, 2010

Kenneth Snelson, **B-Tree II**, 2005

FREDERIK MEIJER GARDENS AND SCULPTURE PARK 1000 East Beltline NE, Grand Rapids, MI 49525
INFO (616) 957-1580; www.meijergardens.org   **ARTISTS** Magdalena Abakanowicz, Nina Akamu, Hanneke Beaumont, Jonathan Borofsky, Louise Bourgeois, Deborah Butterfield, Edgar Degas, Jim Dine, Mark di Suvero, Andy Goldsworthy, Keith Haring, Barbara Hepworth, Richard Hunt, Dietrich Klinge, Alexander Liberman, Jacques Lipchitz, Aristide Maillol, Igor Mitoraj, Henry Moore, Juan Muñoz, Manuel Neri, Louise Nevelson, Claes Oldenburg and Coosje van Bruggen, Carolyn Ottmers, Mimmo Paladino, Arnaldo Pomodoro, George Rickey, Auguste Rodin, Kenneth Snelson, Bill Woodrow   **SCULPTURES** 160
REFERENCES Antenucci Becherer, Joseph. *Gardens of Art: The Sculpture Park at the Frederik Meijer Gardens*. Grand Rapids, MI: Frederik Meijer Gardens and Sculpture Park, 2002.

Frederik Meijer Gardens and Sculpture Park

Grand Rapids, Michigan

The Frederik Meijer Gardens and Sculpture Park were created to explore the relationship between art and nature. They now house more than 160 sculptures on more than 132 acres of indoor and outdoor gallery space located just a few minutes' drive from downtown Grand Rapids.

In 1995 the West Michigan Horticultural Society and Lena and Frederik Meijer came up with the idea of creating a space to display the Meijers' collection in a botanical garden. The park opened seven years later with an initial group of twenty-four sculptures by modern and contemporary artists, and it has continued to expand. The project's aim is to create an encyclopedic collection that covers different eras and does not repeat or overlap with works currently held in other collections in the area.

The works in the permanent collection are located in two sites. The sculpture park and gallery collection is divided between indoor and outdoor installations, based on each work's size and materials. More than thirty sculptures are exhibited in the park; most are figurative, although some abstract sculptures are on display. *The Kiss* by Auguste Rodin and *Dancer* by Edgar Degas are exhibited in the Victorian garden, as well as works by Aristide Maillol, Jacques Lipchitz, Henry Moore, Louise Nevelson, Mark di Suvero, Magdalena Abakanowicz, George Rickey, Claes Oldenburg and Coosje van Bruggen, Juan Muñoz, Hanneke Beaumont, Louise Bourgeois, and Mimmo Paladino. The second area is composed of gardens (some seasonal-themed and dotted with playful animal sculptures) and greenhouses.

Every year a sculpture competition brings in new artists whose work is displayed alongside the permanent collection.

Andy Goldsworthy, **Grand Rapids Arch**, 2001–05

Magdalena Abakanowicz, **Figure on a Trunk**, 1998

Type A, **Team Building (Align)**, 2010

100 ACRES: THE VIRGINIA B. FAIRBANKS ART AND NATURE PARK Indianapolis Museum of Art, 4000 Michigan Road, Indianapolis, IN 46208 **INFO** (317) 923-1331; www.imamuseum.org/100acres **ARTISTS** Atelier Van Lieshout, Kendall Buster, Jeppe Hein, Alfredo Jaar, Los Carpinteros, Tea Mäkipää, Mary Miss, Type A, Visiondivision, Andrea Zittel **SCULPTURES** 10 **REFERENCES** Blake, Edward L., and Marlon Blackwell, *100 Acres: The Virginia B. Fairbanks Art and Nature Park,* Indianapolis, IN: Indianapolis Museum of Art, 2010.

100 Acres: The Virginia B. Fairbanks Art and Nature Park

Indianapolis Museum of Art, Indianapolis, Indiana

This new park, which sits on one hundred acres of woods, fields, and lakes, opened in 2010 alongside the Indianapolis Museum of Art (IMA). The park was designed to stimulate and increase understanding and awareness of nature through art and vice versa. Its creation was overseen by Lisa Freiman, curator of contemporary art at the IMA, who aimed to develop a space that would welcome all kinds of visitors rather than something overly precious.

With this goal in mind, works were created only on commission, with each artist assigned a specific site within the park. All the sculptures are open to interaction. Visitors are meant to picnic inside some of them, such as *Funky Bones* (2010) by Atelier Van Lieshout; play basketball in others, as with *Free Basket* (2010) by Los Carpinteros; or meditate in works such as *Park of the Laments* (2010) by Alfredo Jaar. Also ripe for exploration is Andrea Zittel's inhabitable living structure *Indy Island*, a capsule situated in the middle of a lake, where visitors are invited to adjust living conditions to their individual needs. *Team Building (Align)* by Type A is designed to interact with the natural elements. Formed by two steel rings hung from telephone poles, it plays with light as it changes with the seasons; the shadows of the two rings line up exactly on the summer solstice. The most recent work, added in 2012, is the Swedish architecture firm Visiondivision's *Chop Stick,* an outdoor pavilion for resting and relaxing created out of the trunk of a single tree.

Andrea Zittel, **Indy Island**, 2010

Jeppe Hein, **Bench Around the Lake**, 2010

Tom Sternal, **Cage Form**, 1990

Kuenz Sculpture Park

Cedarhurst Center for the Arts, Mount Vernon, Illinois

Cedarhurst Center for the Arts was founded in 1973 with the opening of the Mitchell Museum on approximately ninety acres of land owned by John R. and Eleanor Mitchell, philanthropists and art collectors who bequeathed their property and art to the local community.

Kuenz Sculpture Park was created in 1992. At first, the park exhibited the work of local artists only, but today it is more international in flavor. It is also increasingly high-profile due to a series of long-term loans and to its close work with gallery owners and artists, who receive funding from the museum for the installation and upkeep of the sculptures.

The park has kept the original lush plants, trees, and other natural elements that provided shelter from the outside world when it was still private property. Particularly lovely is Martha Enzmann's sculpture *Dancers* (1993–94), two anthropomorphic figures connected by a thread that float on the surface of a lake and move in the wind, and the site-specific installation *Self-Suspended/Fallen* by Alfio Bonanno, which garnered much attention for the park. On long-term loan is *Untitled* by Keith Haring. Known best for his paintings, this iconic artist of the 1980s created this group of large-scale sculptures depicting three babies in blue, yellow, and red aluminum.

Martha Enzmann, **Dancers**, 1993–94

KUENZ SCULPTURE PARK Cedarhurst Center for the Arts, 2600 Richview Road, Mount Vernon, IL 62864
INFO (618) 242-1236; www.cedarhurst.org   **ARTISTS** Aldon Addington, Jonathan Auger, Tova Beck-Friedman, Fletcher Benton, Philippo Bermani, Alfio Bonanno, Chakaia Booker, Dee Christy Briggs, Ned Cain, Cosimo Cavallaro, Rico Eastman, Bob Emser, Martha Enzmann, Linda Fleming, Harry Gordon, Keith Haring, Michael Helbing, Kathleen Holmes, Bruce Johnson, Ann Jon, Howard Kalish, John Kearney, Judy Sutton Kracke, Alexander Liberman, Pat McDonald, Scott McMillin, Jerry Monteith, Konried Muench, Robin Murez, Dennis Oppenheim, Beverly Penn, Douglas Ross, Foon Sham, Eric Shaw, Tom Sternal, Gunnar Theel, Robert Youngman, Andy Zimmermann, Glenn Zweygardt **SCULPTURES** 60

Andy Zimmermann, **Crossroads**, 1994

(top) View of the park from above; (bottom) Spencer Finch, **Lunar**, 2011

Millennium Park and the Bluhm Family Terrace

Chicago, Illinois

Millennium Park combines art, architecture, and landscape design in a single urban space inaugurated in July 2004. Born of a partnership between the City of Chicago and the local community, it is intended to display work by internationally recognized artists, architects, and landscape architects.

The Jay Pritzker Pavilion, designed by architect Frank Gehry, hosts the Grant Park Music Festival and other events and concerts year-round. It was named for Jay Pritzker, the Chicago businessman who founded the prestigious Pritzker Architecture Prize with his wife, Cindy, in 1979; Gehry received the prize in 1989. Gehry is also responsible for the bridge that connects Millennium Park with Daley Bicentennial Plaza. The bridge offers a panoramic view of the Chicago skyline, Grant Park, and Lake Michigan, as well as creating a sound barrier for the park.

Crown Fountain was commissioned from Spanish artist Jaume Plensa and is an excellent addition to the city's public art collection. Two glass towers with LED screens on their faces stand over a pool and project images of passersby.

Lurie Garden was designed by landscape architects Gustafson Guthrie Nichol Ltd, Piet Oudolf, and Robert Israel. Its inspiration is the motto *Urbs in Horto* ("city in a garden"), in reference to Chicago's transformation into a lush and green city.

Cloud Gate, an elliptical steel sculpture shaped like a cloud and inspired by liquid mercury, was the first open-air public installation by British artist Anish Kapoor in the United States. An arch serves as an entryway into a concave space located under the sculpture, where visitors to the park are invited to enter and touch the work and admire the images reflected on its surface.

The four Exelon Pavilions, designed according to stringent sustainability criteria, are the site of recreational activities and house the welcome center and the entrance to the parking area. The two southern pavilions, designed by Renzo Piano, are part of the expansion of the Art Institute of Chicago, the city's major museum, founded in 1893. The new plan adds exhibition spaces for modern and contemporary art collections and green spaces and gardens connecting the buildings, which can be used for open-air exhibits of art.

One of these spaces is the Bluhm Family Terrace, a panoramic terrace that faces Millennium Park and the Chicago skyline. It hosts rotating exhibits, the first of which was dedicated to Scott Burton; in 2011 Pae White's *Restless Rainbow* transformed the space into a stage for art and was itself a work of art, while in 2012 Spencer Finch's *Lunar* explored the relationship between space and light.

MILLENNIUM PARK AND THE BLUHM FAMILY TERRACE 201 E. Randolph Street, Chicago, IL 60602 **INFO** (312) 742-1168; www.millenniumpark.org **ARTISTS** Scott Burton, Spencer Finch, Anish Kapoor, Jaume Plensa, Pae White **LANDSCAPE DESIGN** Kathryn Gustafson, Robert Israel, Piet Oudolf **ARCHITECTURE** Frank Gehry, Renzo Piano **REFERENCES** Gilfoyle, Timothy J. *Millennium Park: Creating a Chicago Landmark.* Chicago: University of Chicago Press, 2006.

(top) Donald Lipski, **Ball? Ball! Wall? Wall!**, 1994; (bottom) Mary Miss, **Pool Complex: Orchard Valley**, 1983–85

Laumeier Sculpture Park

St. Louis, Missouri

According to its official documentation, "Laumeier Sculpture Park expands the context of contemporary sculpture beyond the traditional confines of a museum. It is Laumeier's mission to initiate a lifelong process of cultural awareness, enrich lives, and encourage creative thinking by actively engaging people in experiences of sculpture and nature simultaneously."

Laumeier Sculpture Park was created in the late 1960s, when Matilda Laumeier bequeathed land to the County Department of Parks of St. Louis in memory of her husband, Henry. A few years later, the open-air museum was inaugurated. Today it houses more than seventy-five works of art, most of them large in size, site specific, and focused on the relationship between art and nature.

The sculptures are surrounded by plants and trees, installed along paths that weave through wooded and open areas. The entrance to the north is marked by *St. Louis Project* (1989) by Richard Fleischner. There are works by Ernest Trova (including one of his series of *Falling Man* sculptures, which is also visible from the entrance), who initiated the sculpture collection by giving the then-new park forty works. Sculptures by Judith Shea, Terry Allen and Anthony Caro are located in the museum, an early twentieth-century Tudor-style building. On the museum lawn, in front of buildings dedicated to exhibits and research, stand *Intricate Wall* (2001–04) by Sol LeWitt, on loan from the LeWitt Collection; and *Destino* (2003) by Mark di Suvero.

With *Pool Complex: Orchard Valley* (1983–85), Mary Miss created a site-specific work by manipulating natural elements and a preexisting pool. Interest in ecological themes led to the installation in the 1990s of work such as *Four Shades* (1994) by Ian Hamilton Finlay and the botanical installation *Hortus Obscurus (The Dark Garden)* (1996) by Frances Whitehead. The nature trails that run through the wooded areas of the park lead past *Untitled* (1988–89), by Ursula von Rydingsvard, an orderly composition of volumes in wood, and *Cromlech Glen* (1985–90) by Beverly Pepper, two earth pyramids covered in grass and with wooden stairways running up their faces.

Other site-specific installations include *Face of the Earth #3* (1988) by Vito Acconci, a sculpted face with its features dug out of the ground to create a walkable space. The open spaces of the park offer larger works that incorporate natural elements, such as *Crete* (1976–78) by Charles Ginnever, *The Way* (1972–80) by Alexander Liberman, *Untitled* (1984) by Donald Judd, and *Compression Line* (1968) by Michael Heizer.

LAUMEIER SCULPTURE PARK 12580 Rott Road, St. Louis, MO 63127
INFO (314) 615-5278; http://laumeiersculpturepark.org/   **ARTISTS** Vito Acconci, Terry Allen, Arman, Charles Arnoldi, Harriet Bart, Jonathan Borofsky, Anthony Caro, Robert Chambers, Mark di Suvero, Walter Dusenbery, Dale Eldred, Johann Feilacher, Jackie Ferrara, Ian Hamilton Finlay, Richard Fleischner, Linda Fleming, Charles Ginnever, Ronald Gonzalez, Dan Graham, George Greenamyer, Michael Heizer, Jene Highstein, Jenny Holzer, Richard Hunt, Jerald Jacquard, Donald Judd, William King, Sol LeWitt, Alexander Liberman, Donald Lipski, Robert Lobe, John Mason, Mark Mennin, Mary Miss, Robert Morris, Davis Nash, Manuel Neri, Karyn Olivier, Beverly Pepper, George Rickey, Tony Rosenthal, Alison Saar, Niki de Saint Phalle, Judith Shea, Valeska Soares, Robert Stackhouse, Michael Steiner, Steve Tobin, Ernest Trova, Ursula von Rydingsvard, David von Schlegell, Frances Whitehead, Isaac Witkin   **SCULPTURES** 75   **REFERENCES** Ferrara, Jackie. *Laumeier Sculpture Park: Ten Sites: Works, Artists, Years.* St. Louis, MO: Laumeier Sculpture Park and Museum, 1992; Brown, Susan M., George McCue, Beej Nierengarten-Smith, and Laumeier Sculputure Park. *Laumeier Sculpture Park: Second Decade, 1987–1996.* St. Louis, MO: Laumeier Sculpture Park and Museum, 1998.

Vito Acconci, **Face of the Earth III**, 1988

Jene Highstein, **Ada's Will**, 1990

Isamu Noguchi, **California Scenario**, 1980–82

California Scenario

Costa Mesa, California

Isamu Noguchi's *California Scenario* is a landscape-design gem located in the business district of Costa Mesa. It is bordered by the glass walls of two skyscrapers and a white concrete wall. Built from 1980 to 1982, it stands as an abstract representation of the California landscape and carefully balances opposing elements: nature and artifice, water and stone, light and shadow, geometric forms and organic shapes. The path that winds through the garden, which has a sandy surface that is uniform throughout the space, passes through several different environments, all native to Noguchi's birth state of California. There's *Desert Land,* with a horizon combined with a sand dune planted with cactus. *Forest Walk* represents cool, shaded, wooded areas. Numerous symbolic references to water include a canal that runs from the sculptural *Water Source* across the entire garden and ends in a granite volume, *Water Use,* which is both the end point and the starting point for a new cycle.

Sculptural groups of stones punctuate the space and emphasize the size of the entire composition. Though the garden is small, its elements, volumes, colors, textures, and plays of light and shadow seem to make it bigger, providing an abstract edge and moving its (physical and mental) horizon beyond the white wall that surrounds it. As Valerie Fletcher writes in *Isamu Noguchi: Master Sculptor,* "In his late carvings and garden environments Noguchi achieved subtle and sophisticated syntheses of nature with the man-made, fusing organic and geometric, balancing intuition with intellect. *California Scenario* seamlessly integrates them. Although it is an enclosed space adjacent to an office building, *California Scenario* appears open and spacious; the proportional relationship of the asymmetric pyramid to the smaller rocks and plants creates a sense of vastness and scale beyond the actual dimensions of the garden."

Isamu Noguchi, **California Scenario**, 1980–82

CALIFORNIA SCENARIO 611 Anton Boulevard, Costa Mesa, CA 92626
INFO www.noguchi.org   **ARTISTS** Isamu Noguchi   **DESIGN** Isamu Noguchi

Topher Delaney, **Garden Play**, 2009

Cornerstone Gardens

Sonoma, California

Cornerstone Gardens (also known as Cornerstone Place since 2007) are among the most innovative art gardens and the first of their kind opened in the United States.

In 2004, founder Chris Hougie opened these gardens, modeling them on the International Garden Festival in Chaumont-sur-Loire in France. About twenty gardens occupy nine acres of land, each one designed by a landscape architect for the purpose of linking architecture, art, and nature. Asked to create concept gardens (permanent installations representing a cross between landscape design and art), the artists were given wide-ranging creative freedom and open-air rooms in which to work.

The landscape architects and artists involved in the project created experimental spaces, in some cases using landscape-design elements, often repeating them to form a sequence. Ken Smith used this technique with *Daisy Border,* as did Andy Cao and Xavier Perrot with *Cocoons.* Other artists created playful spaces, such as Martha Schwartz's *The Usual Suspects* and Land-I Archicolture's *Stone's Throw.* Still others played off the ambiguity between the natural and the artificial, including Claude Cormier with his *Blue Tree.* Others created true environmental installations, such as Walter Hood and Alma Du Solier with *Eucalyptus Soliloquy,* Andy Cao and Xavier Perrot with *Lullaby Garden,* and Andrea Cochran. Yoji Sasaki created *The Garden of Visceral Serenity,* while environmental artist Topher Delaney designed *Garden Play.*

Andy Cao and Xavier Perrot, **Lullaby Garden**, 2004

CORNERSTONE GARDENS 23570 Arnold Drive, Sonoma, CA 95476
INFO (707) 933-3010; www.cornerstonegardens.com   **ARTISTS** Marco Antonini, Tom Balsley, Pamela Burton, Roberto Capecci, Andy Cao and Xavier Perrot, Rios Clementi, Andrea Cochran, Claude Cormier, Topher Delaney, Alma Du Solier, Rios Clementi Hale Studio, Walter Hood, Land-I Archicolture, David McCrory, Moore Iacofano Goltsman Inc., Roger Raiche, Yoji Sasaki, Mario Schjetnan, Martha Schwartz, Raffaella Sini, Ken Smith, James van Sweden and Sheila Brady, Peter Walker **SCULPTURES 18**

Claude Cormier, **Blue Tree**, 2004

Yoji Sasaki, **The Garden of Visceral Serenity**, 2004

Olympic Sculpture Park

Olympic Sculpture Park

Seattle, Washington

Olympic Sculpture Park began as an urban space for contemporary art and cultural initiatives and a joint project of the Seattle Art Museum and the Trust for Public Land. Its construction was a sixty-five-million-dollar project that started in 1999 and ended with the opening to the public in 2007. The project was handled by New York firm Weiss/ Manfredi. Dug out of an industrial site of approximately ten acres on the Seattle waterfront, the park zigzags among the area's urban infrastructure facilities, the railroad, and a four-lane highway.

"Olympic Sculpture Park establishes a creative dialogue with infrastructure (railway, road approach, waterfront promenade), making it an active part of the project. Not all interventions to existing city infrastructure elements have to involve burying them or dispensing with them entirely; in some cases, this course of action will be essential, but in others these elements can become feature of the whole." (Joan Busquets, "The Urban Impact," in *Olympic Sculpture Park for the Seattle Art Museum,* Harvard Graduate School of Design).

The park serves as connective tissue between the city and the water, with pathways and bridges that link green spaces to urban spaces in a fluid succession of natural and artificial shapes. Plants are local and native to the Pacific Northwest. Seven cement walls surround the grass lawns and paved areas that house large sculptures. Seventeen permanent works have been installed, including *Wake* (2004) by Richard Serra, *Eagle* (1971) by Alexander Calder, *Neukom Vivarium* (2004–06) by Mark Dion, and *Father and Son* (2004–05) by Louise Bourgeois, a fountain that marks the entrance to the park.

A multiuse pavilion of approximately three thousand square meters provides a site for events year-round, contributing to the multifunctional character of this urban space.

The pavilion

OLYMPIC SCULPTURE PARK 2901 Western Avenue, Seattle, WA 98121
INFO (206) 654-3100; www.seattleartmuseum.org   **ARTISTS** Louise Bourgeois, Alexander Calder, Anthony Caro, Mark Dion, Mark di Suvero, Teresita Fernández, Ellsworth Kelly, Roy McMakin, Louise Nevelson, Claes Oldenburg and Coosje van Bruggen, Roxy Paine, Beverly Pepper, Richard Serra, Tony Smith   **SCULPTURES** 25
ARCHITECTURE AND LANDSCAPE DESIGN WEISS/MANFREDI Architecture/Landscape/Urbanism
REFERENCES Manfredi, Michael, and Marion Weiss. *Weiss/Manfredi: Surface/Subsurface.* New York: Princeton Architectural Press, 2007.

Olympic Sculpture Park

LEARNING SPACES

View of the museum and sculpture garden from the northeast

Abby Aldrich Rockefeller Sculpture Garden

Museum of Modern Art, New York, New York

The Abby Aldrich Rockefeller Sculpture Garden in the Museum of Modern Art (MoMA) has existed since the museum's inception.

Located in midtown Manhattan, it is one of the premier examples of garden design in an urban context. Created in 1939 with funds donated by John D. Rockefeller Jr. (one of the museum's three founders), this garden gave rise to the tradition of American museums exhibiting their sculpture collections in open spaces, true open-air galleries, in direct contact with natural or urban elements.

The garden was designed a few weeks after the museum opened by director Alfred H. Barr Jr. and architecture curator John McAndrew, based on an organic design that was quite different from the one that exists today. The current garden (dedicated to Abby Aldrich Rockefeller, the wife of John D. Rockefeller Jr.) reflects a 1953 design by Philip Johnson, at the time director of the museum's Department of Architecture.

The expanded MoMA, which reopened in 2004 in a new building designed by Japanese architect Yoshio Taniguchi, maintained the original space, emphasizing the important role of the garden and making it the focal point for the entire architectural composition. The garden is a rectangular courtyard slightly below street level and separated from the street by a wall. It is characterized by a linear composition of horizontal planes in gray and white marble, two rectangular pools, and carefully arranged plantings. In the aggregate, these elements create a space of physical and visual relaxation among the urban density of Fifty-Fourth Street, which runs alongside the garden.

There is no specific order recommended for enjoying the works in the garden. Indeed, Johnson's design seems to ask each visitor to explore the sculptures, the open space, and the many views of surrounding buildings freely, pausing in various spots.

The works here are of different sizes, materials, and eras. The earliest works exhibited were from figurative artists. These include Aristide Maillol's *The River* (1938–43), facing the water in one of the two pools, and *The Mediterranean* (1902–05); Gaston Lachaise's *Standing Woman* (1932); and works by Auguste Rodin and Henri Matisse. Later, the outdoor collection was expanded through the addition of sculptures in other styles, including Alexander Calder's *Black Widow* (1950), Pablo Picasso's *She-Goat* (1950), Anthony Caro's *Midday* (1960), David Smith's *Cubi X* (1963), and Claes Oldenburg's *Geometric Mouse, Scale A* (1975).

The garden's spatial potential makes it particularly suited to housing temporary exhibits of contemporary art, as it has over the years. These have included exhibits of Richard Serra's environmental installations, Doug Aitken's videos, and other architecture and design subjects.

ABBY ALDRICH ROCKEFELLER SCULPTURE GARDEN Museum of Modern Art, 11 West 53rd Street, New York, NY 10019 **INFO** (212) 708-9400; www.moma.org **ARTISTS** Doug Aitken, Scott Burton, Alexander Calder, Anthony Caro, Max Ernst, Katharina Fritsch, Gaston Lachaise, Jacques Lipchitz, Aristide Maillol, Henri Matisse, Elie Nadelman, Claes Oldenburg, Tom Otterness, Pablo Picasso, Auguste Rodin, Richard Serra, David Smith, Tony Smith **ROTATING EXHIBITS** **ARCHITECTURE** Yoshio Taniguchi (2004 expansion) **LANDSCAPE DESIGN** John McAndrew; Philip Johnson (partially redesigned by Yoshio Taniguchi **REFERENCES** Reed, Peter. *A Modern Garden: The Abby Aldrich Rockefeller Sculpture Garden at The Museum of Modern Art.* New York: Museum of Modern Art, 2007.

The Abby Aldrich Rockefeller Sculpture Garden, 2004

Mike and Doug Starn, **Big Bambú: You Can't, You Don't, and You Won't Stop**, The Metropolitan Museum of Art, 2010

Iris and B. Gerald Cantor Roof Garden

Metropolitan Museum of Art, New York, New York

Every year, from May through October, the Metropolitan Museum of Art's roof garden features a new installation by a contemporary artist. Dedicated to Iris and B. Gerald Cantor, the roof garden is one of several spaces in the museum that have resulted from the donations of this philanthropic couple. They were art collectors, primarily of the work of Auguste Rodin, and their names are linked to other museums, including the Los Angeles County Museum of Art—which also has a sculpture garden named for them—and the Brooklyn Museum.

This open-air room is approximately 9,700 square feet and sits atop the Lila Acheson Wallace Wing, which houses modern art. Exhibits in the roof garden have been dedicated to many internationally well-known artists over the last decade, including Magdalena Abakanowicz (1999), David Smith (2000), Joel Shapiro (2001), Claes Oldenburg and Coosje van Bruggen (2002), Roy Lichtenstein (2003), Andy Goldsworthy (2004), Sol LeWitt (2005), Cai Guo-Qiang (2006), Frank Stella (2007), Jeff Koons (2008), Roxy Paine (2009), Mike and Doug Starn (2010), and Anthony Caro (2011).

Visitors enjoy a splendid view of Central Park; when Christo and Jeanne-Claude's *The Gates* was installed in the park in February 2005, the roof terrace was opened in February, outside of its usual schedule, so that people could view the project from this excellent vantage point. The latest work as of this writing, *Cloud City* (2012), was created by Argentine artist Tomás Saraceno specifically for the roof garden. This piece consisted of transparent interconnected modules joined to create a walk-through residential habitat inspired by eco-urban utopias seeking a sustainable answer to the issues of contemporary living. It merged art, architecture, science, and technology.

IRIS AND B. GERALD CANTOR ROOF GARDEN Metropolitan Museum of Art, 1000 Fifth Avenue, New York, NY 10028-0198 **INFO** (212) 535-7710; www.metmuseum.org **ARTISTS** Magdalena Abakanowicz, Anthony Caro, Christo and Jeanne-Claude, Andy Goldsworthy, Sol LeWitt, Roy Lichtenstein, Jeff Koons, Roxy Paine, Cai Guo-Qiang, Claes Oldenburg and Coosje van Bruggen, Tomás Saraceno, Joel Shapiro, David Smith, Mike and Doug Starn, Frank Stella **ROTATING EXHIBITS**

Roxy Paine, **Maelstrom**, 2009

Ball-Nogues, **Liquid Sky**, 2007

MoMA PS1

Long Island City, New York

PS1 was founded in 1971 by Alanna Heiss as the Institute for Art and Urban Resources. Over thirty years this center for contemporary art has become increasingly important in the national and international scene because of its independent approach. It eventually became affiliated with the Museum of Modern Art (MoMA) in 2000.

Located in Long Island City, not far from the Noguchi Museum and Socrates Sculpture Park, its name is an abbreviation for Public School Number 1, because the turn-of-the-century building where it is housed was once a public school. In 1997 the museum reopened after a three-year renovation, with new spaces designed by Frederick Fisher of Los Angeles.

PS1 does not have a permanent collection, but it exhibits some semipermanent work, including the James Turrell skyspace *Meeting* (1986) on the third floor. The outdoor spaces, a visually appealing series of open-air galleries surrounded by cement walls, are ideal for performances, outdoor exhibits, and site-specific installations, which are held mostly in the summer months. In 1999 Philip Johnson designed a temporary pavilion for events—the first project handled in conjunction with MoMA.

The Young Architects Program is an annual competition held by PS1 and MoMA with the goal of selecting new work to be placed in the garden during the center's summer events. The winning projects, which have combined landscape design, urban design, and environmental installations to various degrees, have included *Percutaneous Delights* (1998) by Gelatin, *Dunescape* (2000) by ShoP, *subWave* (2001) by ROY, *Playa Urbana/Urban Beach* (2002) by William E. Massie, *Light-Wing* (2003) by Tom Wiscombe of EMERGENT, *Canopy* (2004) by nARCHITECTS, *SUR* (2005) by Xefirotarch, *BEATFUSE!* (2006) by OBRA, *Liquid Sky* (2007) by Ball-Nogues, *P.F.1. (Public Farm One)* (2008) by WORK Architecture Company, *afterparty* (2009) by MOS, *Pole Dance* (2010) by Solid Objectives–Idenburg Liu, and *Holding Pattern* (2011) by Interboro Partners. HWKN won the 2012 competition with *Wendy,* which explores the theme of interaction between the environment and architecture; this sculptural filter will clean the air of pollution equivalent to the exhaust from 260 cars.

MoMA PS1 22-25 Jackson Avenue, Long Island City, NY 11101
INFO (718) 784-2084; http://momaps1.org/ **ARTISTS** Ball-Nogues, EMERGENT, Gelatin, HWKN, Interboro Partners, MOS Architects, nARCHITECTS, OBRA, ROY, SHoP, Solid Objectives–Idenburg Liu, William E. Massie, James Turrell, WORK Architecture Company, Xefirotarch **ROTATING EXHIBITS**

Sculptures in the main quad by Nova Mihai Popa, Sandy Macleod, Walter Channing

Pratt Institute Sculpture Park

Brooklyn, New York

This park is part of the renowned Pratt Institute, an art and design school founded in Brooklyn's Fort Greene neighborhood in 1887. Located in an urban residential area, the school's campus is composed of former commercial buildings that have been transformed into classrooms; the garden surrounds them. A wall runs around the garden, and there are four main entrances. Entering through one of them, visitors immediately encounter *Love*, one of Robert Indiana's most famous sculptures, in its original Cor-Ten steel version.

The sculpture garden and the nearby park form a small green oasis in the neighborhood. Students relax and study in the garden, which also serves as a public space, open to area residents until evening. Each year, fifty works are installed on the campus. These are loans from well-known and emerging artists, students, and the school's staff; works are also commissioned by curators. They are distributed on all the open areas: the lawn, courtyards, and walls of buildings. Many artists visit the campus to choose the best site for installation of their work. Among the better-known sculptors with work at Pratt are Tony Rosenthal, George Sugarman, Donald Lipski, Mark di Suvero, Siah Armajani, and Ilan Averbuch, and in the past, works by Charles Ginnever, Ursula von Rydingsvard, and Sol LeWitt have been exhibited.

The sculptures are of different sizes, made from different materials, and speak different languages, forming a varied collection that represents the exploration that goes on both inside and outside academic environments.

Raphael Zollinger, **Welcome**, 2005

PRATT INSTITUTE SCULPTURE GARDEN 200 Willoughby Avenue, Brooklyn, NY 11205
INFO (718) 636-3600; www.pratt.edu   **ARTISTS** Siah Armajani, Ilan Averbuch, Fletcher Benton, Walter Channing, Mark di Suvero, Tom Doyle, Mel Edwards, Kathleen Gilrain, Charles Ginnever, Joel Graesser, Philip Grausman, Robert Indiana, Adella Karclova, William King, Grace Knowlton, Sol LeWitt, Donald Lipski, Peter Lundberg, Sandy Macleod, Sung Ha No, Nova Mihai Popa, Tom Otterness, Joel Perlman, Robert Ressler, Tony Rosenthal, Frank Sanson, George Sugarman, Bernar Venet, Martha Walker, Arthur Weyhe, Ursula von Rydingsvard, Raphael Zollinger   **SCULPTURES** 59

Richard Serra, **Stacks**, 1990

Margaret and C. Angus Wurtele Sculpture Garden and Susan Morse Hilles Sculpture Courtyard

Yale University Art Gallery, New Haven, Connecticut

The Yale University Art Gallery, founded in 1832, is housed in a building designed by Louis I. Kahn during the period when he was teaching at Yale (1947–57) and built from 1951 to 1953. It was the first modern building added to the university campus. A 2006 renovation highlighted the original architectural detail and created two open-air exhibit spaces.

The first of these is the Susan Morse Hilles Sculpture Courtyard, a sunken patio visible from the street through two vertical cuts in the wall that surrounds it. The only work exhibited is the Richard Serra installation *Stacks* (1990), which was initially commissioned by the gallery as a site-specific work for the sculpture hall in the Egerton Swartwout–designed Gothic wing of the gallery that sits adjacent to Kahn's building. Following the renovation, the artist himself designed the new installation in the open space on the patio. Composed of two rectangular rusted-metal volumes placed one in front of the other and vertically sunk into the pavement along the central axis of the courtyard, the work creates a metaphysical landscape and defines and enhances the complex architectural space that surrounds it.

The second open space in the gallery is the Margaret and C. Angus Wurtele Sculpture Garden, enlarged and enhanced with a donation from the philanthropic couple for whom it is named. This donation also provided the funds to purchase Martin Puryear's *Le Prix* (2006), located in the small paved courtyard that serves as the first level of the garden. Directly accessible from the north side through the gallery's lobby, the Wurtele Sculpture Garden sits on two different levels and is visually and physically connected to the gallery's first two floors, which offer a direct view of its works and natural background through large windows that run floor to ceiling. This combination of natural elements, installed sculptures (about ten from the permanent collection rotate in the garden), and surrounding architecture enhances the garden's visual and spatial complexity.

Though the gallery is the only building at Yale with what can strictly be defined as a sculpture garden, the Yale campus has many carefully positioned installations and sculptures in its open spaces, plazas, and gardens. One of the most evocative in its combination of architecture and sculpture is the Beinecke Rare Book and Manuscript Library (1963) and the area that surrounds it. Designed by seasoned architect Gordon Bunshaft (also the creator of the Hirshhorn Museum and Sculpture Garden in Washington, DC) and working with Isamu Noguchi, the library consists of one aboveground building resting on a horizontal plane, with underground public spaces below. These include a reading room and offices that face Noguchi's sculpture courtyard, formally known as the Courtyard Garden for Beinecke Library (1960–64). This courtyard is almost invisible from the plaza above, but it provides spatial, architectural, and material continuity with the building. The courtyard is paved with a single slab of marble. On it rest three sculptures in primary geometric shapes—circle, pyramid, cube—that form a cerebral and artificial landscape in its entirety.

MARGARET AND C. ANGUS WURTELE SCULPTURE GARDEN Yale University Art Gallery, 1111 Chapel Street, New Haven, CT 06510 **INFO** (203) 432-0600; www.artgallery.yale.edu **ARTISTS** Gordon Bunshaft, Paul Forte, Louise Nevelson, Isamu Noguchi, Martin Puryear, Richard Serra, Joel Shapiro, David Smith, Tony Smith, William Tucker **SCULPTURES** 10 **ARCHITECTURE** Louis I. Kahn

Louise Nevelson, **Transparent Horizon**, 1975

List Visual Arts Center Outdoor Collection

Massachusetts Institute of Technology, Cambridge, Massachussetts

Managed by the Massachusetts Institute of Technology (MIT) List Visual Arts Center, this outdoor art collection is dispersed around the university campus. It's one of the best collections of its kind, with more than fifty sculptures, and it merges art and architecture. Many of the sculptures engage in dialogue with complex buildings such as the university chapel, designed by Eero Saarinen in 1955 with an altar by Harry Bertoia and a sculptural bell tower by Theodore Roszak.

The List Visual Arts Center (named in honor of patrons Albert and Vera List) is located on the east side of the campus in the Wiesner Building. *Reclining Figure* (1963) by Henry Moore, originally intended for New York City's Lincoln Center for the Performing Arts, lies near *Figure Découpée* by Pablo Picasso. The Green Building, another signature building on the campus, is home to the monumental sculptures *La Grande Voile* (1965) by Alexander Calder and *Transparent Horizon* (1975) by Louise Nevelson. Beverly Pepper's *Trinity* (1971) is installed in an open courtyard adjacent to the Compton Laboratories, designed by Gordon Bunshaft in 1955, next to the Ray and Maria Stata Center, a 2004 design from Frank Gehry.

In the large Killian Court are two sculptures installed symmetrically in relation to the neoclassical building around them: *Three-Piece Reclining Figure, Draped* (1976) by Henry Moore and *Guennette* (1977) by Michael Heizer.

Moving westward, the campus offers a series of works of modern architecture: the MIT Chapel faces the Kresge Auditorium (1954), also by Saarinen, and not far away stands the Baker House (1949) by Alvar Aalto.

At the western border of the campus is the New House Dormitory (1979) by Josep Lluis Sert with the outdoor sculpture *For Marjorie* (1961) by Tony Smith, and farther to the north is Simmons Hall (2002) by Steven Holl, with the Dan Graham installation *Yin/Yang Pavilion* (2003).

LIST VISUAL ARTS CENTER OUTDOOR COLLECTION Massachusetts Institute of Technology, 20 Ames Street, Building E15, Atrium Level, Cambridge, MA 02139 INFO (617) 253-4680; http://listart.mit.edu
ARTISTS Alvar Aalto, David Bakalar, Jennifer Bartlett, Herbert L. Beckwith, Pietro Belluschi, Harry Bertoia, Edwin H. Blashfield, Émile-Antoine Bourdelle, Gordon Bunshaft, Victor Burgin, Scott Burton, Alexander Calder, Eduardo Catalano, Mark di Suvero, Harold Eugene Edgerton, Jackie Ferrara, Frank Gehry, Dan Graham, Dimitri Hadzi, Michael Heizer, Candida Höfer, Steven Holl, Jean Robert Ipoustéguy, Sol LeWitt, Jacques Lipchitz, James Melchert, Henry Moore, Elizabeth Murray, Walter Netsch, Louise Nevelson, John Newman, Jorge Pardo, I. M. Pei, Beverly Pepper, Pablo Picasso, Matthew Ritchie, Kevin Roche, Auguste Rodin, Theodore Roszak, Eero Saarinen, James Sanborn, Nicolas Schöffer, Josep Lluis Sert, Tony Smith, Frank Stella, Hugh Stubbins, Sara Sze, Ralph Thomas Walker, William Welles Bosworth, Gary Wiley, Isaac Witkin SCULPTURES 80

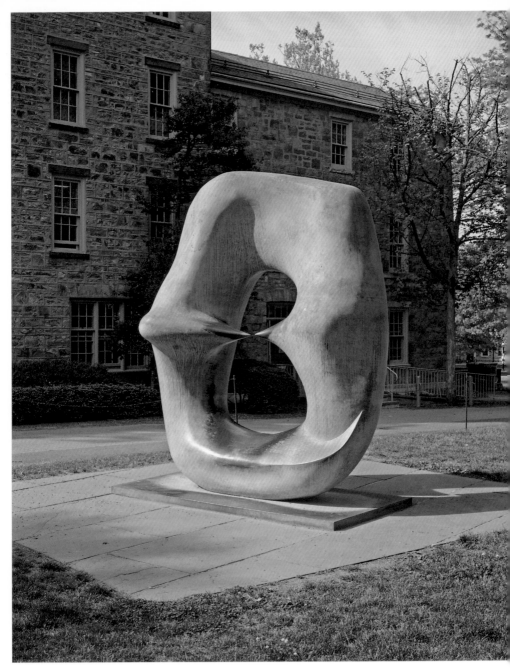

Henry Moore, **Oval with Points**, 1969–70

John B. Putnam Jr. Memorial Collection

Princeton University, Princeton, New Jersey

The John B. Putnam Jr. Memorial Collection is a collection of sculptures arranged in open spaces on the campus of Princeton University, near the university's major buildings. The collection is named for a Princeton student who died in World War II. Funds were donated anonymously in 1964 for the creation of a collection of twentieth-century sculpture, which was established in 1969 and 1970 by a committee of art and museum experts (Alfred H. Barr Jr., director of the Museum of Modern Art; Thomas P. F. Hoving, director of the Metropolitan Museum of Art; P. Joseph Kelleher, director of the Princeton University Art Museum; and William M. Milliken, director of the Cleveland Museum of Art).

The initial collection consisted of twenty pieces. Some of the first works exhibited in the university's garden are parts of well-known series, such as *Atmosphere and Environment X* (1969–70) by Louise Nevelson, at one of the entrances, and *Cubi XIII* (1963) by David Smith. *Oval with Points* (1968) by Henry Moore was inspired by an elephant skull that scientist Sir Julian Huxley and his wife, Juliette, brought back from Africa as a gift for the artist; fascinated by the object, Moore reproduced its shape with two ovals that just barely touch at their ends and are pointed like tusks. Alexander Calder's *Five Disks: One Empty* (1969–70) is a monumental steel sculpture; the artist requested that it be repainted black from its original orange (Princeton's colors are orange and black). The work was created for the campus specifically at Barr's request and installed, standing alone, in Fine Hall Plaza in 1971. Not far from there, Richard Serra's *The Hedgehog and the Fox* (2000) creates spaces in movement silhouetted against the curved walls of the new Lewis Library designed by Frank Gehry. *Head of a Woman* by Pablo Picasso, in front of Spelman Halls (dormitories designed by I. M. Pei), is a large-scale reproduction of a 1962 maquette by the artist, assembled in 1971 by Norwegian artist Carl Nesjar, who acted as the intermediary between Picasso and the Putnam Collection.

JOHN B. PUTNAM JR. MEMORIAL COLLECTION Princeton University Art Museum, Princeton, NJ 08544
INFO (609) 258-3788; www.princetonartmuseum.org   **ARTISTS** Reg Butler, Alexander Calder, Jacob Epstein, Naum Gabo, Michael Hall, Gaston Lachaise, Jacques Lipchitz, Clement Meadmore, Henry Moore, Masayuki Nagare, Louise Nevelson, Isamu Noguchi, Eduardo Paolozzi, Antoine Pevsner, Pablo Picasso, Arnaldo Pomodoro, George Rickey, Richard Serra, David Smith, Tony Smith, Kenneth Snelson   **REFERENCES** AAVV. *Sculpture of Princeton University Press*, John B. Putnam Memorial Collection. Princeton, NJ: Princeton University Art Museum, 1982.

John Ruppert, **Orb**, 2009

Janet and Alan Wurtzburger
and Ryda and Robert H. Levi Sculpture Gardens

Baltimore Museum of Art, Baltimore, Maryland

The Baltimore Museum of Art has two sculpture gardens that are green oases in the heart of downtown Baltimore. They contain thirty-five sculptures that are part of the museum's collection. The gardens are named for two philanthropic couples who donated their collections to the museum to make them accessible to a wider public: the Janet and Alan Wurtzburger Sculpture Garden is a terraced garden next to the museum's entrance, while the Ryda and Robert H. Levi Sculpture Garden is a quiet, intimate space to the side of the building.

The Wurtzburger Sculpture Garden, opened in 1980, faces the entrance to the museum and is set on a series of terraces that recall exhibit galleries, crossed by a pool of water and surrounded by a cement wall that physically and psychologically sets the garden apart from the street. The donated works include *Three-Piece Reclining Figure No.1* (1961–62) by Henry Moore, positioned picturesquely at the entrance to the garden; *Fruit* (1911) by Émile-Antoine Bourdelle; *Endless Ribbon* (1953) by Max Bill, a reinterpretation of a Möbius strip in marble; a mobile by José Ruiz de Rivera titled *Construction 140* (1971); the monumental *Spitball* (1961) by Tony Smith; *Tauromachy* (1953) by Germaine Richier; *Man Walking* (1952) by Fritz Wotruba; *May 1940: The Destroyed City* (1957) by Ossip Zadkine; an installation intended for public use (meaning visitors are invited to sit on it and interact with it) by Scott Burton titled *Rock Chair* (1986–87); *Sheila's Song* (1982) by Anthony Caro; *Mother and Child, II* (1941–43) by Jacques Lipchitz; *The Miracle* (1954) by Marino Marini; *Head* (1974) by Joan Miró; and *Untitled* (1958) by Isamu Noguchi.

In contrast with the formal Wurtzburger garden, where sculptures are exhibited in a proper outdoor gallery, the nearby Levi Sculpture Garden, opened in 1988, is an informal space, lush with vegetation, where a path leads visitors to discover works installed amid nature and arranged on green lawns. The sculptures are mostly from the second half of the twentieth century and include *Eight-Part Circle* (1976/1987) by Michael Heizer; *Untitled* (1986) by Ellsworth Kelly; *Sister Lu* (1978–79) by Mark di Suvero; *Sculpture 74* (1974) by Phillip King; *Seventh Decade Forest* (1971–76) by Louise Nevelson; and, lastly, two monumental works that dominate the garden: the Alexander Calder stabile *100 Yard Dash* (1969) and *Space Churn with Spheres, Variation III* (1972) by George Rickey.

In 2009, the sculpture *Orb* by John Ruppert, from a series of installations made with chain-link fence, was added to the collection after Ruppert won the prestigious Mary Sawyers Baker Prize.

JANET AND ALAN WURTZBURGER AND RYDA AND R. H. LEVI SCULPTURE GARDENS The Baltimore Museum of Art, 10 Art Museum Drive, Baltimore, MD 21218-3898 **INFO** (443) 573-1700; www.artbma.org
ARTISTS Max Bill, Émile-Antoine Bourdelle, Scott Burton, Alexander Calder, Anthony Caro, Mark di Suvero, Michael Heizer, Ellsworth Kelly, Philip King, Jacques Lipchitz, Marino Marini, Joan Miró, Henry Moore, Louise Nevelson, Isamu Noguchi, Germaine Richier, George Rickey, José Ruiz de Rivera, Auguste Rodin, John Ruppert, Tony Smith, Fritz Wotruba, Ossip Zadkine **SCULPTURES** 35

Hirshhorn Museum and Sculpture Garden

HIRSHHORN MUSEUM AND SCULPTURE GARDEN 700 Independence Avenue SW, Washington, DC 20560
INFO (202) 633-4674; www.hirshhorn.si.edu   **ARTISTS** Alexander Archipenko, Arman, Jean Arp, Saul Baizerman,
Leonard Baskin, Émile-Antoine Bourdelle, Alexander Calder, Anthony Caro, Tony Cragg, Willem de Kooning, Jacob
Epstein, Barry Flanagan, Lucio Fontana, Elisabeth Frink, Pablo Gargallo, Alberto Giacometti, Dimitri Hadzi, Barbara
Hepworth, Richard Hunt, Jean Robert Ipoustéguy, Ellsworth Kelly, Gaston Lachaise, Henri Laurens, Jacques
Lipchitz, Aristide Maillol, Giacomo Manzù, Marino Marini, Raymond Mason, Henri Matisse, Joan Miró, Henry Moore,
Juan Muñoz, Reuben Nakian, Claes Oldenburg, Pablo Picasso, Germaine Richier, Auguste Rodin, Judith Shea,
David Smith, Tony Smith, Kenneth Snelson, Paul Suttman, William Tucker, Fritz Wotruba, Francisco Zúñiga
SCULPTURES 65   **ARCHITECTURE** Gordon Bunshaft   **REFERENCES** Fletcher, Valerie J. *A Garden for Art: Outdoor
Sculpture at the Hirshhorn Museum.* Washington, DC: Hirshhorn Museum and Sculpture Garden, 1998.

Hirshhorn Museum and Sculpture Garden

Washington, DC

The Hirshhorn Museum and Sculpture Garden is located on the National Mall, the area in Washington, DC, that is home to the country's major cultural institutions. The museum was founded by Joseph Hirshhorn, an entrepreneur in the mining industry and an art collector who in 1966 decided to donate his collection to the Smithsonian Institution. Thus the Hirshhorn Museum was created. A circular building with an almost completely solid exterior face, it is a pure form raised on monumental *pilotis*. Architect Gordon Bunshaft conceived of the building as "a large piece of functional sculpture" where art could be exhibited "without architectural distractions." The building sits in a plaza, where visitors encounter the first group of sculptures displayed in and around the museum. The monolithic building interacts with large-scale works like *Two Discs* (1965) by Alexander Calder, one of the artist's stabiles; *Needle Tower* (1968) by Kenneth Snelson, a spatial geometric composition five stories high inspired by the work of Buckminster Fuller; and *Spatial Concept: Nature* (1959–60) by Lucio Fontana, a group of five spherical sculptures resting on the grass, which the artist intended to be displayed in a natural, open space.

The sculpture garden in the museum (first opened in 1974 and reopened in 1981 after renovation by the landscape architect Lester Collins, who highlighted its original beauty and made it a small jewel of a "park within the park") directly faces the National Mall and houses about sixty sculptures dating from 1880 to 1960. An integral part of the museum, the garden contains many of the approximately 144 sculptures that previously were exhibited on the lawns of Round Hill Estate, the private residence of Joseph Hirshhorn. Developed on different levels and below the level of the National Mall, the garden marks the museum's underground galleries and is enhanced by natural elements and by a reflecting pool in its center. This is the location of the group *Burghers of Calais* (1884–89) by Auguste Rodin, which stands next to other works by Rodin and many human figures by Aristide Maillol, Émile-Antoine Bourdelle, Henri Matisse, Gaston Lachaise, Pablo Picasso, Giacomo Manzù, Henry Moore, Marino Marini, and Alberto Giacometti. Also in the garden are Barbara Hepworth's anthropomorphic *Figure for Landscape* (1960), whose carved-out spaces frame the surrounding landscape; Joan Miró's fantastic character *Lunar Bird* (1944–46); Jean Arp's ambiguous *Evocation of a Form: Human, Lunar, Spectral* (1950), which evokes different forms depending on the viewpoint; Henry Moore's *Three-Piece Reclining Figure No. 2: Bridge Prop* (1963) and *Two-Piece Reclining Figure: Points* (1969–70), variations on the motif of the reclining figure that the artist explored so thoroughly throughout his career, and *Three-Way Piece No. 3: Vertebrae (Working Model)* (1968), which references the skeletal structures he collected. Among the abstract works are the Alexander Calder mobile *Six Dots over a Mountain* (1956), anchored on a stable base. Also present are the David Smith works *Cubi XII* (1963), from the group of twenty-eight sculptures the artist created from 1961 to 1965 whose surfaces are designed to interact with light and color from the surrounding countryside, and *Voltri XV*. The latter work is from a different series by the artist, consisting of twenty-six sculptures he created in an abandoned factory in Voltri in the summer of 1962, using materials found at the site.

Hector Guimard, **An Entrance to the Paris Metropolitan**, 1902–13

NATIONAL GALLERY OF ART SCULPTURE GARDEN 4 Constitution Avenue NW, Washington, DC 20565
INFO (202) 737-4215; www.nga.gov **ARTISTS** Magdalena Abakanowicz, Jean Arp, Louise Bourgeois, Scott
Burton, Alexander Calder, Mark di Suvero, Max Ernst, Barry Flanagan, Andy Goldsworthy, Hector Guimard,
Ellsworth Kelly, Sol LeWitt, Roy Lichtenstein, Aristide Maillol, Henry Moore, Joan Miró, Isamu Noguchi, Claes
Oldenburg and Coosje van Bruggen, George Rickey, James Rosati, Lucas Samaras, Joel Shapiro, David
Smith, Tony Smith, Frank Stella **SCULPTURES** 25 **LANDSCAPE DESIGN** Laurie D. Olin/Olin Partnership
ARCHITECTURE John Russell Pope; I. M. Pei; Skidmore, Owings & Merrill (Pavilion Café)

National Gallery of Art Sculpture Garden

Washington, DC

The National Gallery of Art Sculpture Garden opened in 1999, thirty years after it was first conceived. The garden was designed by Olin Partnership and features a pavilion designed by Skidmore, Owings & Merrill. It houses ten sculptures acquired specifically for the space, seven from the permanent collection, and others that are on loan.

The garden directly faces the National Mall and can be accessed through six different entrances. No specific route is meant to be followed; walking or relaxing in one of the many pleasant spots in the garden, one can observe pop-art sculptures by Claes Oldenburg and Coosje van Bruggen—*Typewriter Eraser and Scale X* (1999), gigantic versions of everyday objects—or the unusual *House I* (1996/1998) by Roy Lichtenstein, a two-dimensional reproduction of a house on a grand scale. Then there's Sol LeWitt's modern Mesopotamian ziggurat *Four-Sided Pyramid* (1999); a complex and delicate play on balance made with eight tons of linear steel elements, Mark di Suvero's *Aurora* (1992–93); the geometric compositions of Joel Shapiro's *Untitled* (1989); David Smith's *Cubi XXVI* (1965); Tony Smith's *Moondog* (1964/1998–99); and George Rickey's kinetic sculpture *Cluster of Four Cubes* (1992). Ellsworth Kelly provides an environmental installation, *Stele II* (1973), while Barry Flanagan offers a variation (albeit an ironic one) of Rodin's famous *Thinker*—*Thinker on a Rock* (1997). Seating motifs are offered by Scott Burton with his *Six-Part Seating* (1985/1998), an invitation to art as participation, and the dreamlike vision of Lucas Samaras's *Chair Transformation Number 20B* (1996). Louise Bourgeois contributes an image of female fragility and maternal protection with her *Spider* (1996), while Magdalena Abakanowicz's thirty immobile, headless children's bodies, *Puellae* (*Girls*) (1992) recall deportations from Poland to Germany under the Nazi regime. The surreal *Gothic Personage, Bird-Flash* (1974) is a sculpture that Joan Miró made late in life. Also from 1974 is Alexander Calder's *Cheval Rouge* (*Red Horse*), one of his large-scale stabiles, many of which are located in public spaces and have become urban landmarks.

Finally, there is *An Entrance to the Paris Métropolitan* (1902/1913) by Hector Guimard. This Art Nouveau symbol merging organic shapes and technical engineering still decorates eighty or so Paris subway-station entrances. In this sculpture garden on the National Mall in Washington, it stands as a metaphorical exit from the imaginative and surreal landscape that is home to these seventeen sculptures.

There are many sculptures on the open spaces next to the two buildings that form the National Gallery—the neoclassical West Building, designed by John Russell Pope, and the East Building, an I. M. Pei masterpiece. Henry Moore's enormous bronze *Knife Edge Mirror Two Piece* (1976–78), installed at the entrance to the East Wing, participates in the architectural composition of the space, balancing with its sinuous mass the vacuum created in the face of the large glass entrance. Arranged on the lawn that surrounds the building are Jean Arp's *Oriform* (1962), Tony Smith's *The Snake is Out* (1992), and Frank Stella's *Prinz Friedrich von Homburg, Ein Schauspiel, 3X* (1998–2001); on the North Terrace is *Untitled* (1977) by James Rosati. In 2005, English artist Andy Goldsworthy was commissioned by the National Gallery to make a site-specific sculpture (*Roof*), to be installed in the open space on the ground floor of the East Building, which had at first been occupied by a reflecting pool and later was refashioned into a garden for exhibits on the theme of landscape. The installation consists of nine domes, a shape the artist has employed since the 1970s and a clear reference to the architecture that predominates in the city of Washington, DC.

Melvin Charney, **Esplanade Ernest-Cormier**, 1989

Esplanade Ernest-Cormier

Canadian Centre for Architecture, Montreal, Quebec

The Canadian Centre for Architecture (CCA), founded in 1979 and opened to the public in 1989, houses an extraordinary collection of research materials on architecture, as well as half a million items, including books, drawings, prints, models, and photographs.

The CCA takes up an entire city block in the center of Montreal. It consists of a late nineteenth-century building, Shaughnessy House, with a modern wing designed by the Rose + Guggenheimer Studio. The CCA Garden, officially the Esplanade Ernest-Cormier, was conceived as a metaphorical representation of the CCA as a museum and research center dedicated to architecture. Visibly echoing the center's history, the garden connects the surrounding buildings with their architectural legacy and evokes the narrative tradition of the great classic gardens.

Located on one side of Boulevard René-Lévesque, the garden is laid out in a series of six rooms, each one linked to a specific period in the history of the site: the Orchard, the Meadow, the Arcade (which mirrors the facade of the Shaughnessy House from the other side of the street), the Esplanade, the Belvedere, and the Allegorical Columns, containing eleven works, each with an allegorical-architectural motif.

Melvin Charney, the internationally known artist and architect behind the project, describes the garden as the synthesis of three categories: the urban garden (an "urban event" that relates to other elements of the city), the museum garden (an open-air room whose relationship to visitors is through architectural elements), and the neighborhood garden (an episodic place where both constructed and planted spaces can be enjoyed).

ESPLANADE ERNEST-CORMIER Canadian Centre for Architecture, 1920 Rue Baile, Montreal, Quebec, H3H 2S6, Canada   **INFO** (514) 939-7026; www.cca.qc.ca   **ARTISTS** Melvin Charney **SCULPTURES** 11   **REFERENCES** Richards, Larry. *Canadian Centre for Architecture: Buildings and Gardens.* Cambridge, MA: MIT Press, 1989.

(top) Mark di Suvero, **Yes! For Lady Day**, 1968–69; (bottom) Mary Miss, **Field Rotation**, 1981

Nathan Manilow Sculpture Park

Governors State University, University Park, Illinois

Located on the campus of Governors State University in an area of the Midwest characterized by vast, open prairies, the Nathan Manilow Sculpture Park is one of the few in the region that focuses on work from the 1960s and 1970s; it exhibits about thirty large-scale sculptures. The park was created in the late 1960s, founded by Lewis Manilow and named for his father, Nathan, a businessman who built the postwar towns of Park Forest and University Park in Chicago.

The first work in the park, *Yes! For Lady Day,* was commissioned from Mark di Suvero and built over the course of two years (1968–69). During this period, the campus became a place for artists to meet, and they were invited and welcomed by Lewis Manilow to his farm (today the park's conference center).

A 1976 exhibit titled *The Sculptor, the Campus, and the Prairie* brought to the campus some pieces that have since become part of the permanent collection, such as *Icarus* (1975) by Charles Ginnever, *Illinois Landscape No. 5* (1976) by John Henry, *Outgrown Pyramid II* and *Large Planar Hybrid* (1973–74) by Richard Hunt, and *Falling Meteor* (1975) by Jerry Peart.

In the early 1980s, environmental works were commissioned, including the site-specific *Field Rotation* (1981) by Mary Miss, *Flying Saucer* (1977) by Jene Highstein, and the land-art piece *Bodark Arc* (1982) by Martin Puryear.

House Divided (1983) by Bruce Nauman was built directly on the campus as a permanent work and from the outside resembles the typical rural structures on the prairies of the Midwest.

In recent years, the park has held outdoor solo exhibits and added to its collection with new works. These include *Working on the Failed Utopia* (2005), created by Christine Tarkowski in cooperation with the Art-in-Architecture Program of the State of Illinois. Tarkowski used a spatial structure to transform images of everyday objects (in this case, photographs of garbage found near her studio) into an aesthetic statement.

Christine Tarkowski, **Working on the Failed Utopia**, 2005

NATHAN MANILOW SCULPTURE PARK Governors State University, 1 University Parkway, University Park, IL 60484 **INFO** (708) 534-4486; www.govst.edu/sculpture/ **ARTISTS** Mike Baur, James Brenner, Mark di Suvero, Michael Dunbar, Ted Sitting Crow Garner, Charles Ginnever, John Henry, Jene Highstein, Richard Hunt, Terrence Karpowicz, Henri Etienne-Martin, Clement Meadmore, Mary Miss, Bruce Nauman, John Payne, Jerry Peart, Martin Puryear, Richard Rezac, Joel Shapiro, Edvins Strautmanis, Christine Tarkowski, Tony Tasset, Dan Yarbrough **SCULPTURES** 26 **REFERENCES** Schjeldahl, Peter and Nathan Manilow Sculpture Park. *The Nathan Manilow Sculpture Park.* University Park, IL: Governors State University Foundation, 1987.

Minneapolis Sculpture Garden

Minneapolis Sculpture Garden and Outdoor Galleries

Walker Art Center, Minneapolis, Minnesota

The Minneapolis Sculpture Garden opened in 1988 on eleven acres of public green space. The plaza and walking paths of the garden, one of the largest urban sculpture gardens in the United States, host contemporary sculptures by American and foreign artists. The garden sits next to the Walker Art Center, opened in the early 1900s and expanded in the 1940s with a collection of modern art made possible by a donation from Mrs. Gilbert Walker. The center handles artists' programs, exhibits, and works of art for the garden.

The Walker Art Center as it exists today was built based on a design by American architect Edward Larrabee Barnes from 1966 to 1971, with an addition by the same architect in 1984. From 1986 to 1988, Barnes worked on designing the Minneapolis Sculpture Garden. The architect planned open-air galleries like museum spaces, with clearly defined rooms to explicate the relationship between the works rather than simply juxtaposing them. This led him to design a formal space modeled on the Tivoli Gardens in Italy, comprising four rooms revolving around a system of orthogonal axes, surrounded by hedges and visible from the museum. In the center is a pop-art sculpture by Claes Oldenburg and Coosje van Bruggen, *Spoonbridge and Cherry* (1985–88), which has become a symbol of the city. Elsewhere in the garden are *Octopus* (1964) and *The Spinner* (1966) by Alexander Calder, *Molecule* (1977–83) by Mark di Suvero, and *Without Words* (1988) by Judith Shea, as well as monumental installations by Richard Serra, Ellsworth Kelly, and Tony Smith. In 1993 the garden was expanded by landscape architect Michael Van Valkenburgh to create new spaces, the Arlene Grossman Memorial Arbor and the Flower Garden to the north.

A pedestrian bridge (the Irene Hixon Whitney Footbridge, 1988) designed by the artist Siah Armajani connects the Minneapolis Sculpture Garden with Loring Park. The nearby Cowles Conservatory exhibits Frank Gehry's *Standing Glass Fish* (1986). A second expansion by Herzog & de Meuron opened in 2005 and took the form of a group of boxlike buildings with large windows that open to the outside spaces and an urban square inspired by the sculpture garden.

MINNEAPOLIS SCULPTURE GARDEN AND OUTDOOR GALLERIES Walker Art Center, 1750 Hennepin Avenue, Minneapolis, MN 55403 **INFO** (612) 375-7600; http://garden.walkerart.org **ARTISTS** Magdalena Abakanowicz, Kinji Akagawa, Siah Armajani, Saul Baizerman, Scott Burton, Deborah Butterfield, Alexander Calder, Tony Cragg, Mark di Suvero, Barry Flanagan, Frank Gehry, Charles Ginnever, Dan Graham, Brower Hatcher, Jene Highstein, Jenny Holzer, Ellsworth Kelly, Georg Kolbe, Philip Larson, Charlie Lazor, Sol LeWitt, Jacques Lipchitz, Giacomo Manzù, Marino Marini, Henry Moore, Reuben Nakian, David Nash, Louise Nevelson, Isamu Noguchi, Claes Oldenburg and Coosje van Bruggen, Martin Puryear, George Segal, Richard Serra, Judith Shea, Jonathan Silver, Tony Smith, Richard Stankiewicz, Jackie Winsor **SCULPTURES** 40 **LANDSCAPE DESIGN** Edward Larrabee Barnes; Michael Van Valkenburgh **ARCHITECTURE** Edward Larrabee Barnes; Herzog & de Meuron **REFERENCES** Sorenson, Mary Eileen, and Jacqueline Copeland. *Minneapolis Sculpture Garden: A Collaboration Between the Walker Art Center and the Minneapolis Park and Recreation Board.* Minneapolis, MN: Walker Art Center, 1998.

Jaume Plensa, **Nomade**, 2007

Greenwood Park and John and Mary Pappajohn Sculpture Park

Des Moines Art Center, Des Moines, Iowa

The Des Moines Art Center is a museum specializing in contemporary art. The complex is composed of three buildings facing Greenwood Park that are cleverly connected to each other. It was created in 1948, based on a design by Eliel Saarinen, and was expanded twenty years later with an addition by I. M. Pei. As the museum's collection grew in the 1970s and 1980s, it became necessary to expand the museum again, especially due to the increased presence of large works of contemporary art. That addition was designed by Richard Meier. The park runs around all three buildings and is particularly suited to sculptures that interact with both natural and architectural elements. For example, *Animal Pyramid* (1990) by Bruce Nauman is a composition of zoomorphic shapes located in a sheltered spot adjacent to a wing of the museum, while *Standing Stones* by Richard Serra is a series of granite blocks that punctuate a section of the park, attracting the eye and expanding the viewer's horizons to include the surrounding landscape. On an even larger scale is Andy Goldsworthy's on-site work *Three Cairns,* made with the large sandstone mounds that the artist has been using since the 1980s. This is part of a series intended to connect distant points in the United States: the Des Moines Art Center, which houses the first installation; the San Diego Museum of Contemporary Art in La Jolla (the second); and the Neuberger Museum in Purchase, New York (the third).

With *Greenwood Pond: Double Site,* Mary Miss is working on transforming the landscape in an entire area of the park, including a lake, in order to make it more user-friendly.

In fall 2009, a second sculpture park opened at the Downtown Art Center, created through a partnership among the Des Moines Art Center; the city; private donors; and collectors John and Mary Pappajohn, who donated sixteen works and whose name the park bears. The first group of work is composed of sculptures by Louise Bourgeois, Scott Burton, Deborah Butterfield, Anthony Caro, Tony Cragg, Willem de Kooning, Mark di Suvero, Barry Flanagan, Ellsworth Kelly, Martin Puryear, Richard Serra, Joel Shapiro, Judith Shea, Tony Smith, William Tucker, and Yoshitomo Nara (who contributed one of the most recent installations).

John and Mary Pappajohn Sculpture Park

GREENWOOD PARK AND JOHN AND MARY PAPPAJOHN SCULPTURE PARK Des Moines Art Center, 13th Street and Grand Avenue, Des Moines, IA 50312 **INFO** (515) 277-4405; www.desmoinesartcenter.org **ARTISTS** Louise Bourgeois, Scott Burton, Deborah Butterfield, Anthony Caro, Tony Cragg, Mark di Suvero, Barry Flanagan, Richard Fleischner, Andy Goldsworthy, Ellsworth Kelly, Willem de Kooning, Mary Miss, Henry Moore, Yoshitomo Nara, Bruce Nauman, Jaume Plensa, Martin Puryear, Richard Serra, Joel Shapiro, Judith Shea, Tony Smith, William Tucker **ARCHITECTURE** Eliel Saarinen; I. M. Pei; Richard Meier

Louise Bourgeois, **Spider**, 1997

(top) Museum entrance; (bottom) Claes Oldenburg and Coosje van Bruggen, **Shuttlecocks**, 1994

The Kansas City Sculpture Park

Nelson-Atkins Museum of Art, Kansas City, Missouri

The Kansas City Sculpture Park, originally the Henry Moore Sculpture Garden, one of the largest collections of Henry Moore's large-scale works outside of England, is an urban park affiliated with the Nelson-Atkins Museum. The initial area, opened in 1989 and designed by Dan Kiley, sets Moore's sculptures in an idyllic landscape similar to that of the Yorkshire Sculpture Park (which houses the largest open-air collection of this artist's work). The twelve original pieces came from the collection of George Ablah in Tulsa in the late 1980s (eleven of these were acquired by the Hall Family Foundation and one by the City of Kansas City). The Hall Family foundation has since acquired one additional piece by Moore.

In the early 1990s, the museum's Modern Sculpture Initiative undertook a project to transform the Nelson-Atkins Museum into a center for contemporary sculpture. The outdoor collection grew with the addition of large-scale works by Claes Oldenburg and Coosje van Bruggen (*Shuttlecocks,* 1994), Alexander Calder, George Segal, and Isamu Noguchi.

At the same time, a plan to renovate the museum led to construction of the Bloch Building, designed by architect Steven Holl. Five glass structures (known as the "lenses") rise out of the ground and bring light to underground gallery space. A Walter De Maria sculpture, *One Sun/34 Moons* (2002), occupies the entire plaza that lies in front of the entrance to the museum, with thirty-four lenses installed in a pool of water that manipulate natural light and direct it into a parking garage below.

The Bloch Building also has a sculpture garden of its own that faces the sculpture park and is dedicated entirely to the work of Isamu Noguchi.

THE KANSAS CITY SCULPTURE PARK Nelson-Atkins Museum of Art, 4525 Oak Street, Kansas City, MO 64111 **INFO** (816) 751-1278; www.nelson-atkins.org **ARTISTS** Magdalena Abakanowicz, Alexander Calder, Tony Cragg, Walter De Maria, Mark di Suvero, Charles Heit, Gaston Lachaise, Jacques Lipchitz, Henry Moore, Isamu Noguchi, Claes Oldenburg and Coosje van Bruggen, Auguste Renoir, George Rickey, George Segal, Joel Shapiro, Judith Shea, Ursula von Rydingsvard **SCULPTURES** 34 **LANDSCAPE DESIGN** Dan Kiley (The Henry Moore Sculpture Garden) **ARCHITECTURE** Steven Holl Architects **REFERENCES** Scott, Deborah Emont. *The Nelson-Atkins Museum of Art Henry Moore Sculpture Garden.* Kansas City, MO: Trustees of the Nelson Gallery Foundation, 1989; Scott, Deborah Emont, and Martin Friedman. *Modern Sculpture at the Nelson-Atkins Museum of Art: An Anniversary Celebration.* Kansas City, MO: Nelson-Atkins Museum of Art, 1999; Kipnis, Jeffrey, Roland Halbe, and Steven Holl. *Stone and Feather: Steven Holl Architects/The Nelson-Atkins Museum Expansion.* New York: Prestel, 2007.

The Bloch Building at the Nelson-Atkins Museum of Art with Tony Cragg, **Turbo**, 2001

Serge Yourievitch, **La Danseuse Nattova**, 1925

Charles W. Ireland Sculpture Garden

Birmingham Museum of Art, Birmingham, Alabama

The sculpture garden that surrounds the Birmingham Museum of Art is part of a renovation and expansion begun in 1993, which resulted from a partnership between New York sculptor Elyn Zimmerman and architect Edward Larrabee Barnes. It is composed of three different spaces that house both sculptures on loan and those from the permanent collection.

The Red Mountain Garden Area welcomes visitors coming from the museum. This lushly planted area houses the site-specific work *Blue Pools Courtyard* (1993) by artist Valerie Jaudon–two mosaic-tiled reflecting pools created using the Roman *opus sectile* technique. The effect of continuous movement is generated by the colors and materials used and the constantly running water. This area also contains other sculptures, most of them figurative, by Fernando Botero, Auguste Rodin, and Jacques Lipchitz.

The second outdoor space, the Lower Gallery, is an open-air space that is slightly sunken and used for temporary exhibits. These have included work by John Scott, Peer Veneman, Saint Clair Cemin, Luis Jiménez, Zachary Coffin, Tina Haase, Birgit Werres, and Enne Haehnle.

Finally, the Upper Plaza is the site of large-scale sculptures such as the site-specific *Lithos II* by Elyn Zimmerman, a monumental waterfall with a granite pool that forms the eastern wall of the garden, along with works by George Rickey, John Scott, Doug Hollis, Beverly Pepper, and Scott Burton.

Museum entrance

CHARLES W. IRELAND SCULPTURE GARDEN Birmingham Musem of Art, 2000 Rev. Abraham Woods, Jr. Boulevard, Birmingham, AL 35203 **INFO** (205) 254-2565; www.artsbma.org
ARTISTS Fernando Botero, Scott Burton, Anthony Caro, Saint Clair Cemin, Zachary Coffin, Tina Haase, Enne Haehnle, Barbara Hepworth, Doug Hollis, Valerie Jaudon, Luis Jiménez, Sol LeWitt, Jacques Lipchitz, Beverly Pepper, George Rickey, Auguste Rodin, John Scott, Peer Veneman, Birgit Werres, Serge Yourievitch, Elyn Zimmerman
LANDSCAPE DESIGN Elyn Zimmerman **ARCHITECTURE** Edward Larrabee Barnes

Entrance with sculpture by George Segal, **Couple on Two Benches**, 1985

Hunter Museum of American Art Sculpture Garden

Chattanooga, Tennessee

The Hunter Museum Sculpture Garden houses the museum's outdoor collection. It sits on rocky bluffs along the Tennessee River in the city's art district. The external space where the sculptures are exhibited was designed as a pathway connecting the various museum buildings, which are of different eras and in different styles. The Hunter Museum was created in 1952 to house a collection of three thousand pieces of American art and was named for the Hunter family, which founded a Coca-Cola bottling company. The three buildings that currently house the museum include the 1905 mansion in neoclassical style that was the family's original residence, donated upon the death of George Thomas Hunter. In 1973, it was expanded for the first time with the construction of the museum's east wing, a brutalist concrete building. The third building, the west wing, dates to 2005 and was designed and then built to celebrate the original building's one hundredth birthday.

The sculpture park stands among the buildings, and visitors are invited to stroll through and view the fifteen sculptures located at key points, as well as the architecture and the surrounding countryside. Work ranges from monochromatic figures by George Segal, *Couple on Two Benches* (1985), on the terrace of the new west wing to bronzes by Tom Otterness, *Free Money* (2001), at the entrance to the plaza to an equestrian statue by Deborah Butterfield, *Boreal* (2001). Continuing around the border of the museum buildings, visitors encounter figurative sculptures, such as a female figure by Harold Cash, *Mask of D'A-Lal* (1929); the inventive *Weather Watcher* by Jim Collins (1978); and abstract forms such as Alexander Calder's *Pregnant Whale* (1963) and John Henry's *Largo* (1981). The *Hunter Museum Fence* by Albert Paley (1975) and *V-X-II* by Kenneth Snelson (1973–74) were commissioned directly by the museum.

Sculpture plaza

HUNTER MUSEUM OF AMERICAN ART SCULPTURE GARDEN 10 Bluff View Avenue, Chattanooga, TN 37403 **INFO** (423) 267-0968; www.huntermuseum.org **ARTISTS** Terry Allen, Deborah Butterfield, Alexander Calder, Harold Cash, Jim Collins, John Dreyfuss, Brower Hatcher, John Henry, William King, Carol Mickett and Robert Stackhouse, Dennis Oppenheim, Tom Otterness, Albert Paley, George Segal, Kenneth Snelson, John Sugarman, Bart Walter **SCULPTURES** 21

Steve Tobin, **Steel Roots**, 2008

The Patricia and Phillip Frost Art Museum Sculpture Park

Florida International University, Miami, Florida

The idea of creating a sculpture park on the campus of Florida International University emerged during the initial planning stages for the university itself. The purpose was to make art part of the everyday experience of education. The first building on the campus was designed by Albert Sinclair Vrana. Called Primera Casa, it is considered a work of art in and of itself and incorporates sculptural elements into its cement facade. Another work by Vrana is located on the northern wall of the building.

The Art in State Buildings Program is a Florida initiative launched in 1979 to encourage the installation of artwork in public places. It calls for 1 percent of construction costs of state buildings to be used to acquire art for public exhibition in open spaces.

In 1994 the Martin Z. Margulies Collection was loaned to the Frost Museum, which is located on the university campus and oversees the sculpture park. Today, almost all of those sculptures have been returned to their owners, with the exception of one piece that was donated to the museum, *Journey's End* by Ilan Averbuch (1985). Two other pieces were donated to the university: the park's signature piece, *Argosy* (1980) by Alexander Liberman, which is located at the entrance to the campus, and *Marty's Cube* (1983) by Tony Rosenthal, another significant piece.

About thirty works can currently be seen on campus. These include Charles Ginnever's *Forth Bridge* (1979); Anthony Caro's *Caramel* (1975); three sculptures by Jacques Lipchitz; and four by Steve Tobin, including his highly regarded *Steel Roots*.

Steve Tobin, **Steel Roots**, 2002

THE PATRICIA AND PHILLIP FROST ART MUSEUM SCULPTURE PARK Florida International University, 10975 SW 17th Street, Miami, FL 33199   **INFO** (305) 348-2890; http://thefrost.fiu.edu   **ARTISTS** Elisa Arimany, Pablo Atchugarry, Ilan Averbuch, Anthony Caro, Adam Garey, Charles Ginnever, John Henry, Alexander Liberman, Jacques Lipchitz, Emil Lukas, Daniel Joseph Martinez, Barbara Nejina, Joel Perlman, Jean-Claude Rigaud, Tony Rosenthal, STRETCH, Robert Thiele, Steve Tobin, Albert Sinclair Vrana, Jeff Whyman, Arnie Zimmerman   **SCULPTURES** 22

Mark di Suvero, **Ave**, 1973

Dallas Museum of Art Sculpture Garden

Dallas, Texas

The Dallas Museum of Art opened in 1983 in a building designed by Edward Larrabee Barnes. Creation of the museum was one part of a larger urban plan to create an arts district in the city's historic district, close to the Nasher Sculpture Center. The museum is modular, with small courtyards and internal gardens with sculptures, reflecting pools, and lush plant life—all visible from the galleries through large windows.

The sculpture garden is in the southern part of this complex and is accessed from a room in the museum that contains the monumental Claes Oldenburg and Coosje van Bruggen piece *Stake Hitch* (1984).

The garden, designed by Dan Kiley, is a series of open-air rooms segmented with dividing walls and reflecting pools that stand against a background of limestone, providing formal and material continuity with the museum building. Each sculpture is carefully positioned within this geometric complex. Two were commissioned specifically for this space: Ellsworth Kelly's large abstract *Untitled* (1982–83), which overlooks one of the reflecting pools, and Scott Burton's *Granite Settee* (1982–83).

Other works include Barbara Hepworth's two abstract sculptures, *Figure for Landscape* (1960) and *Sea Form (Atlantic)* (1964); Richard Serra's *Untitled* (1971); Richard Long's *Rochechouart Circle* (1990); and Tony Smith's *Willy* (1978). The large empty space at the entrance is balanced by Mark di Suvero's imposing *Ave* (1973), in a bright-red color that contrasts with the stone facade of the building.

The area in and around Dallas and nearby Forth Worth offers numerous cultural attractions and is perhaps one of the best places in the United States in which to view art, architecture, and design in an urban setting. Downtown Dallas features Annette Strauss Square by Foster + Partners; the Dallas Center for Performing Arts by Rem Koolhaas; the John F. Kennedy Memorial by Philip Johnson; and the Morton H. Meyerson Symphony Center by I. M. Pei (together with Dallas City Hall, by the same architect, and Fountain Place, an evocative space designed by Dan Kiley that stands in front of the skyscraper of the same name designed by Henry N. Cobb).

The sculpture garden against the Dallas skyline

DALLAS MUSEUM OF ART SCULPTURE GARDEN 1717 North Harwood Street, Dallas, TX 75201 **INFO** (214) 922-1200; www.dallasmuseumofart.org **ARTISTS** Scott Burton, Mark di Suvero, Barbara Hepworth, Ellsworth Kelly, Richard Long, Aristide Maillol, Henry Moore, Claes Oldenburg and Coosje van Bruggen, Beverly Pepper, Richard Serra, Tony Smith, Kenneth Snelson **SCULPTURES** 20 **LANDSCAPE DESIGN** Dan Kiley **ARCHITECTURE** Edward Larrabee Barnes

Dallas Museum of Art Sculpture Garden

The Nasher Sculpture Garden at the Nasher Sculpture Center

Nasher Sculpture Garden

Nasher Sculpture Center, Dallas, Texas

Raymond D. Nasher created the Nasher Sculpture Center after the death of his wife, Patsy, in order to have a space to exhibit his sculpture collection (which had originally been installed on the couple's private property) on a rotating basis. Nasher commissioned the work in 1999, and the center opened in 2003 in a gallery building designed by Renzo Piano, with an adjacent garden designed by Peter Walker. The museum serves as a kind of urban oasis or "archeological site" (as its creator has deemed it) that stands in contrast to its surrounding modern Dallas environment.

The indoor spaces alternate openings and closures, with glass panels outfitted with a sunscreen that allows in controlled natural light. The three central pavilions contain exhibition galleries, while the two pavilions on the sides contain public spaces and facilities. The garden, enclosed by travertine walls and set a little below street level to create a sheltered space with an intimate feeling, has a spare and linear design. As a result, it feels like a continuation of the covered galleries and enters into a dialogue with them. The three main paths are lined with rows of oak trees that stand on the same horizontal plane on which the artworks are located. The open spaces are shaded by more than 170 trees, including cedars, oaks, myrtles, weeping willows, and magnolias.

The sculptures vary in size, and the collection is rotated, with the number of pieces exhibited at any one time limited by the size of the outdoor space to about twenty-five. These elements were key in designing the landscape and influenced the choice of plantings, the placement of the works themselves, and the complex organizational machinery employed to move them.

The varying sizes of the works (one of the thorniest logistical issues) had a great influence on the design of the garden. Monumental sculptures such as Richard Serra's *My Curves Are Not Mad* (1987), Mark di Suvero's *Eviva Amore* (2001), Alexander Calder's *Three Bollards (Trois Bollards)* (1970), and Richard Deacon's *Like a Bird* (1984) are freestanding on the lawn, while smaller works are showcased using pedestals and other structures. The latter group includes Barbara Hepworth's *Squares with Two Circles (Monolith)* (1963), which is installed in one of the fountains that grace the garden.

The site-specific *Tending, (Blue)* by James Turrell, one of the most recent additions to the garden, is enclosed in a dark-gray cube that contrasts with the artist's typical skyspaces. *Walking to the Sky* (2004) is one of artist Jonathan Borofsky's largest works and features life-size human figures walking along a metal pole toward the sky. Richard Long's installation *Slate Line* (1979) consists of five stones arranged in a straight line end to end. It's part of a large series of works that feature stones in geometric linear, circular, and spiral arrangements, representing nature's unity and man's ability to create order.

NASHER SCULPTURE GARDEN Nasher Sculpture Center, 2001 Flora Street, Dallas, TX 75201 **INFO** (214) 242-5100; www.nashersculpturecenter.org **ARTISTS** Magdalena Abakanowicz, Carl Andre, Jonathan Borofsky, Scott Burton, Alexander Calder, Tony Cragg, Richard Deacon, Mark di Suvero, Raymond Duchamp-Villon, Barbara Hepworth, Donald Judd, Anish Kapoor, Jeff Koons, Roy Lichtenstein, Richard Long, Joan Miró, Henry Moore, Isamu Noguchi, Claes Oldenburg, Martin Puryear, Richard Serra, David Smith, Tony Smith, James Turrell **SCULPTURES** 25 **LANDSCAPE DESIGN** Peter Walker Partners **ARCHITECTURE** Renzo Piano **REFERENCES** Amidon, Jane, and Peter Walker. *Peter Walker and Partners: Nasher Sculpture Center Garden.* New York: Princeton Architectural Press, 2006.

The Nasher Sculpture Garden

Aerial view of the Nasher Sculpture Garden

Wall detail, the Lillie and Hugh Roy Cullen Sculpture Garden

The Lillie and Hugh Roy Cullen Sculpture Garden

Museum of Fine Arts, Houston, Houston, Texas

Designed by Isamu Noguchi and opened in 1986, the Lillie and Hugh Roy Cullen Sculpture Garden originally had been commissioned in 1976 by the Museum of Fine Arts, Houston.

In the 1950s Ludwig Mies van der Rohe had been commissioned to create a development plan for the museum (the original building dates to the 1920s). He came up with a twenty-year expansion plan that would ultimately transform the museum into a veritable campus. He also designed the complex's Cullinan Hall, opened in 1958, and the Brown Pavilion, completed in 1974. (In 2000 the Rafael Moneo–designed Beck Building was also added.)

After Mies's changes were made, a rectangular piece of land was allocated for a new sculpture garden. Noguchi surrounded the area with a series of cement partitions of varying heights, creating an intimate atmosphere that would be sheltered from urban traffic while remaining open. The system of walls defines the space within the garden as well, creating a variety of views as well as marking paths between natural and constructed elements, areas of light and shadow, planted areas and bare soil. The geometry is complex but not invasive and leaves space that can be enjoyed freely by the visitor.

Considered a work of art in its own right, the garden houses a collection of approximately thirty-five sculptures from the museum's permanent collection—from figurative works such as *Flora, Nude* (1910) by Aristide Maillol, *The Walking Man* (1899–1900/1905) by Auguste Rodin, the series *Backs* (1909–30) by Henri Matisse, installed on a wall, and *The Pilgrim* (1939) by Marino Marini to fantastical creatures by Joan Miró such as *Bird* (1968). *Large Standing Woman I* (1960) by Alberto Giacometti was originally intended for One Chase Manhattan Plaza in New York City (the location of Noguchi's *Sunken Garden*) and was inspired by the Gordon Bunshaft's design for the bank's headquarters, while *Quarantania, I* (1947–53/1981) by Louise Bourgeois is one of a group of figures created by the artist in the 1940s. *Spatial Concept, Nature, Nos. 18 & 28* (1959–60) are part of a series of more than thirty spherical sculptures by Lucio Fontana, which the artist began in 1959 and which are usually installed in small groups. *The Crab* (1962) is one of Alexander Calder's colorful stabiles. The abstract sculptures *Two Circle Sentinel* (1961) by David Smith, *Decanter* (1987) by Frank Stella, and *Argentine* (1968) by Anthony Caro were acquired or donated over the years, while other pieces were created specifically for the garden: the site-specific *Houston Triptych* (1986) by Ellsworth Kelly, *Can Johnny Come Out and Play?* (1990–91) by Jim Love, *New Forms* (1991–92) by Tony Cragg, and *The Dance* (2000) by Linda Ridgway.

The garden is also home to more than one hundred species of plants, including maples, mimosas, pine trees, elms, cypresses, magnolias, myrtles, oaks, bamboo, and jasmine chosen by Noguchi with the assistance of landscape architect Johnny Steele.

THE LILLIE AND HUGH ROY CULLEN SCULPTURE GARDEN Museum of Fine Arts, Houston, 1001 Bissonnet Street, Houston, TX 77005 **INFO** (713) 639-7300; www.mfah.org **ARTISTS** Émile-Antoine Bourdelle, Louise Bourgeois, Alexander Calder, Anthony Caro, Tony Cragg, Lucio Fontana, Alberto Giacometti, DeWitt Godfrey, Robert Graham, Joseph Havel, Bryan Hunt, Ellsworth Kelly, Jim Love, Aristide Maillol, Marino Marini, Henri Matisse, Joan Miró, Mimmo Paladino, Linda Ridgway, Auguste Rodin, Joel Shapiro, David Smith, Frank Stella **SCULPTURES** 35 **LANDSCAPE DESIGN** Isamu Noguchi (with Johnny Steele) **ARCHITECTURE** Ludwig Mies van der Rohe, Rafael Moneo **REFERENCES** Greene, Alison de Lima. *Isamu Noguchi: A Sculpture for Sculpture: The Lillie and Hugh Roy Cullen Sculpture Garden.* Houston, TX: The Museum of Fine Arts, Houston, 2006.

Overview of the Lillie and Hugh Roy Cullen Sculpture Garden

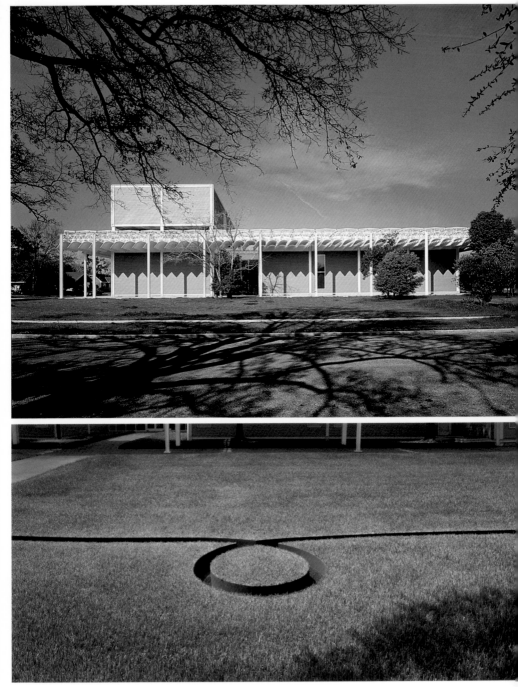

(top) Menil Collection, Renzo Piano Building Workshop and Richard Fitzgerald & Partners;
(bottom) Michael Heizer, **Isolated Mass/Circumflex (#2)**, 1968–72

Loretto Park and Outdoor Sculpture

Menil Collection, Houston, Texas

The Menil Collection, overseen by the Menil Foundation, opened to the public in 1987. It exhibits the private collection of John and Dominique de Menil. The collection consists of more than fifteen thousand pieces from the Paleolithic era to the present, divided into four categories: ancient, Byzantine and Medieval, tribal, and twentieth-century.

The Menils began collecting and exhibiting work in the 1940s, after they moved from France to the United States, and by the 1950s they had already curated well-received exhibits. In the 1970s the collection was made into a permanent exhibit, and Louis Kahn was hired to design a building to house it, but that project never came to fruition due to the death of John Menil followed by that of the architect two years later.

In 1980 Renzo Piano was hired to design the museum. Other spaces were added over the years. In the 1990s the Cy Twombly Gallery, also designed by Piano, was added through a partnership with the Dia Center for the Arts; since 1998 Richmond Hall has housed one of the only two permanent Dan Flavin installations in the United States. The Rothko Chapel, commissioned by the Menils in 1971 and intended to serve as a nondenominational spiritual space for mediation, was designed by Philip Johnson and houses fourteen canvases by abstract expressionist Mark Rothko. The outdoor-sculpture collection in the museum's garden consists of seven pieces: Michael Heizer's *Charmstone* (1991) and *Isolated Mass/Circumflex (#2)* (1968–72), a site-specific work installed on the lawn; Tony Smith's *The Snake is Out* (1962) and, in Loretto Park, the series comprising *The Elevens Are Up* (1963), *Wall* (1964) and *New Piece* (1966); Jim Love's *Jack* (1971), Mark di Suvero's *Bygones* (1976); and Barnett Newman's *Broken Obelisk* (1963–67), installed in a reflecting pool at the entrance to the Rothko Chapel.

LORETTO PARK AND OUTDOOR SCULPTURE Menil Collection, 3900 Yupon Street, Houston, TX 77006 **INFO** (713) 524-9839; www.menil.org; www.rothkochapel.org **ARTISTS** Mark di Suvero, Dan Flavin, Michael Heizer, Jim Love, Max Neuhaus, Barnett Newman, Tony Smith **SCULPTURES** 8 **ARCHITECTURE** Renzo Piano Building Workshop and Richard Fitzgerald & Partners

(top) John Roloff, **Fragment: the Hidden Sea (Island of Refuge)**, 1993; (bottom) Bruce Beasley, **Vanguard**, 1980, in front of Meyer Library

Cantor Arts Center Outdoor Collection

Stanford University, Palo Alto, California

As far back as the early 1900s, the founders of Stanford University felt the campus should include an open-air sculpture collection. Only in the 1960s, however, did the art department begin to systematically install excellent modern sculptures around the campus, intending them to serve as cultural reference points for the Stanford community. In the 1960s the first sculptures in the collection were either acquired or donated, most by the artists. These included Henry Moore's *Large Torso: Arch* (1962–63), donated by Nathan Cummings; Josef Albers's *Stanford Wall* (1980); Alexander Calder's *The Falcon* (1963); Dimitri Hadzi's *Pillars of Hercules III* (1982); Jacques Lipchitz's *Song of the Vowels* (1931); Bruce Beasley's *Vanguard* (1980); Joan Miró's *Bird* (1973); Jack Zajac's *Big Ram Skull and Horn, January* (1976), Auguste Rodin's *Burghers of Calais* (1884–89), and George Segal's *Gay Liberation* (1980). Today, the contemporary art collection includes hundreds of pieces; the campus is also the site of a sculpture garden with sculptures from Papua New Guinea (with approximately forty pieces) and the B. Gerald Cantor Rodin Sculpture Garden at the Cantor Arts Center, a collection that includes about twenty Auguste Rodin bronzes, including *The Gates of Hell* (1880–circa 1980).

In recent years, the art department has continued to work to improve the campus and grow the collection, and also to enhance the interaction between architecture and landscape through site-specific and environmental pieces. More recent additions to the North Lawn of the Cantor Art Center include *Timetable* (2000) by Maya Lin, *Stone River* (2001) by Andy Goldsworthy, *Georgia Granite Circle* (1990) by Richard Long, *Rashomon* (1993–98) by Charles Ginnever, *Call Me Ishmael* (1986) by Richard Serra, and *Fragment: The Hidden Sea (Island of Refuge)* (1993) by John Roloff. The garden of the Center for Clinical Science Research, designed by landscape architect Peter Walker, also houses *Miwok* (1981) by Mark di Suvero.

CANTOR ARTS CENTER OUTDOOR COLLECTION Stanford University, 328 Lomita Drive, Stanford, CA 94305 **INFO** (650) 723-4177; http://museum.stanford.edu **ARTISTS** Josef Albers, Bruce Beasley, Fletcher Benton, J. B. Blunk, Beniamino Bufano, Alexander Calder, William Couper, Aristides Demetrios, Mark di Suvero, Linda Fleming, Antonio Frilli, Charles Ginnever, Andy Goldsworthy, Dimitri Hadzi, Lee Kelly, Maya Lin, Jacques Lipchitz, Richard Long, Larkin G. Mead, Joan Miró, Henry Moore, Tom Otterness, Beverly Pepper, Arnaldo Pomodoro, Antoine Poncet, Auguste Rodin, John Roloff, James Rosati, George Segal, Richard Serra, Kenneth Snelson, François Stahly, William Wetmore Story, Art Thompson, William Turnbull, Meg Webster, Don Yeomans, Jack Zajac **SCULPTURES** 80

Auguste Rodin, **The Walking Man**, 1905

Franklin D. Murphy Sculpture Garden

University of California, Los Angeles, Los Angeles, California

In 1960, Franklin D. Murphy, chancellor of the University of California, Los Angeles, for eight years, decided to build a sculpture garden on the university's campus in an open area then used as a parking lot (and adjacent to the eventual site of the Eli and Edythe Broad Art Center, opened in 2006). The initial collection consisted of thirty-one pieces, which were arranged in a space designed by landscape architect Ralph Cornell; the garden officially opened in 1967.

Today the collection contains seventy-two sculptures by twentieth-century European and American artists. Located in the heart of the university's campus in an informal, open space that welcomes all, especially the university community, the garden is a cross between a typical American museum sculpture garden and an urban park. The garden echoes the regular geometry of the surrounding university buildings, but its center contains more fluid and organic pathways.

The works located in the space connect occasionally with the architecture of the surrounding buildings and with the surrounding landscape. Four Henri Matisse reliefs (1909–30) are installed against the wall of the Broad Center's Wight Art Gallery and run parallel to the facade; *Grande Cretto Nero* (1976–77) by Alberto Burri, a large-scale work donated by the artist, is installed to one side of the Art Center. A series of figures—Auguste Rodin's *The Walking Man* (1905), Aristide Maillol's *Torso* (1938), Henry Moore's *Two-Piece Reclining Figure , No.3* (1961), Émile-Antoine Bourdelle's *Noble Burdens* (1910), Joan Miró's *Mère Ubu* (1975), and Francisco Zúñiga's *Reclining Nude* (1970)—dot the regular grid of the plaza next to the garden. Other pieces are arranged on a lawn accessible through five informal entry points with footpaths between them. The Alexander Calder sculpture *Button Flower* (1959), painted black, is one of his famous stabiles; *Garden Elements* (1962) by Isamu Noguchi (part of a series the artist created in the 1960s that recalls Japanese Zen gardens), is composed of three bronze elements that resemble hills or islands arranged on a horizontal surface that stands in for the landscape.

FRANKLIN D. MURPHY SCULPTURE GARDEN University of California, Los Angeles, 10899 Wilshire Boulevard, Los Angeles, CA 90024 **INFO** (310) 443-7000; www.hammer.ucla.edu **ARTISTS** Oliver Andrews, Alexander Archipenko, Jean Arp, Leonard Baskin, Fletcher Benton, Émile-Antoine Bourdelle, Alberto Burri, Deborah Butterfield, Alexander Calder, Antony Caro, Aldo Casanova, Lynn Chadwick, Leo Cherne, Pietro Consagra, Sorel Etrog, Claire Falkenstein, Eric Gill, Robert Graham, Dimitri Hadzi, Barbara Hepworth, Richard Hunt, Fritz Koenig, Gaston Lachaise, Henri Laurens, Wilhelm Lehmbruck, Jacques Lipchitz, Anna Mahler, Aristide Maillol, Gerhard Marcks, Henri Matisse, Joan Miró, Henry Moore, Robert Müller, Reuben Nakian, Gordon Newell, Isamu Noguchi, George Rickey, Giorgio Amelio Roccamonte, Auguste Rodin, Tony Rosenthal, Richard Serra, David Smith, Francesco Somaini, Louis H. Sullivan, Elden Tefft, George Tsutakawa, William Tucker, William Turnbull, Vladas Vildziunas, Peter Voulkos, Jack Zajac, Wiliam Zorach, Francisco Zúñiga **SCULPTURES** 72 **LANDSCAPE DESIGN** Ralph Cornell **REFERENCES** Burlingham, Cynthia. *The Franklin D. Murphy Sculpture Garden at UCLA*. Los Angeles: Hammer Museum, 2007.

Gerhard Marcks, **Maja**, 1941, in the Franklin D. Murphy Sculpture Garden

Chris Burden, **Urban Light**, 2008, outside the Broad Contemporary Art Museum, designed by Renzo Piano Building Workshop

LOS ANGELES COUNTY MUSEUM OF ART SCULPTURE GARDENS 5905 Wilshire Boulevard, Los Angeles, CA 90036
INFO (323) 857-6000; www.lacma.org   **ARTISTS** Alice Aycock, Chris Burden, Alexander Calder, Anthony Caro, Michael
Heizer, Richard Howard Hunt, Robert Irwin, Donald Judd, Ellsworth Kelly, Jeff Koons, Alexander Liberman, Henry Moore,
Auguste Rodin, Richard Serra, Tony Smith, James Turrell, Peter Voulkos   **SCULPTURES** about 20   **LANDSCAPE DESIGN**
Olin Partnership; Robert Irwin (Palm Garden)   **ARCHITECTURE** Renzo Piano / Renzo Piano Building Workshop (for BCAM)

Los Angeles County Museum of Art Sculpture Gardens

Los Angeles, California

The Los Angeles County Museum of Art (LACMA), located in the city's center, is a museum complex that houses approximately one hundred thousand works of art ranging from ancient to modern. Created in 1910 as the Los Angeles Museum of History, Science and Art, it expanded several times during the twentieth century, and in 1961 it was officially named the Los Angeles County Museum of Art. Organized in various pavilions (the Ahmanson Building for the permanent collection; the Hammer Building for temporary exhibits; the Art of the Americas Building; the Pavilion for Japanese Art; LACMA West), the complex was renovated to reorganize outside spaces and new exhibition spaces. These include the Broad Contemporary Art Museum (BCAM), sponsored by Eli and Edythe Broad, which opened in 2008 in a building designed by the Renzo Piano Building Workshop.

The outdoor spaces, park, and gardens were redesigned at that time to serve as exhibit space for large-scale sculptures. Two installations were present from the start: *Urban Light* by Chris Burden and *Palm Garden* by Robert Irwin. *Urban Light* features 202 cast-iron street lamps from 1920 that once lit the streets of the city of Los Angeles. These have been salvaged, catalogued, restored, and assembled in one work—a piece that has become the signature image of LACMA. Robert Irwin worked closely with Renzo Piano when creating his *Palm Garden* in order to ensure that the grid along which the buildings and garden are laid out would be respected. The project combines art and landscape architecture and is a work in progress, intended to be developed in the coming years, with the goal of creating a botanical garden of palm trees from around the world, integrated with large-scale works.

Michael Heizer's monumental *Levitated Mass* is one of the largest and most complex works installed here (or anywhere else, for that matter). It consists of a slot in the earth constructed on site with a 340-ton monolith balanced over it. Visitors walk through the slot, passing under the enormous mass, a process that forces them to confront its enormous size. Heizer conceived of the piece in the 1960s and only found the right monolith many years later in Riverside County in California.

Open-air pieces added later include James Turrell's *Boullée's Boule* (part of his skyspace series) and *Missed Approach* on the roof terrace of LACMA West; *Train* by Jeff Koons (undergoing a feasibility study) is a replica of a locomotive suspended from a crane, conceptualized as an urban landmark visible from everywhere in the city. The open spaces around the museum are organized in the West Sculpture Garden (on the site of the old garden from the 1960s) and the East Sculpture Garden, which houses twentieth-century pieces, including the Alexander Calder mobile *Three Quintains,* which the museum commissioned in 1964 and which is exhibited in a reflecting pool. Other artists with work here include Alice Aycock, Anthony Caro, Richard Hunt, Donald Judd, Ellsworth Kelly, Alexander Liberman, Henry Moore, Peter Voulkos, and Tony Smith. The gardens were created by the landscape architecture firm Olin Partnership. Richard Serra's *Band* is exhibited on the ground floor of the new Broad Contemporary Art Museum building, and the B. Gerald Cantor Sculpture Garden includes an excellent collection of works by Auguste Rodin.

Fountain at the museum's entrance with Alexander Calder, **Three Quintains**, 1964

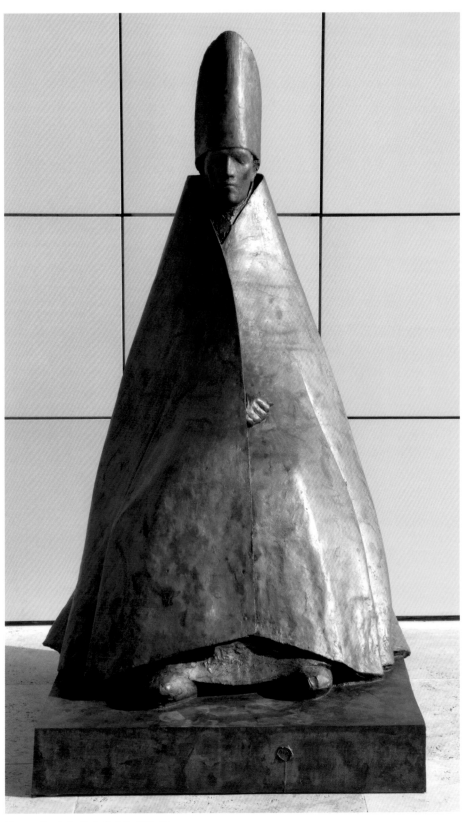

Giacomo Manzù, **Cardinale Seduto**, 1975–77

The Fran and Ray Stark Sculpture Garden and the Central Garden

Getty Center, Los Angeles, California

The Getty Center in the Los Angeles hills preserves the artistic legacy of J. Paul Getty as well as being a highly regarded international center for arts research. From a picturesque hillside, the center overlooks the western part of the city. The complex was designed by Richard Meier, who worked with Olin Partnership on the landscape architecture. The complexity of the surrounding landscape inspired an equally sophisticated series of rooms that alternate private areas (for research and for the center's administrative offices) and public areas where visitors can admire not just the art collection itself, but the natural beauty of the location. (The promenade that winds up the hill where the center is located is truly spectacular; it offers a view of the entire city, the Santa Monica Mountains, and the ocean.)

The outdoor sculpture collection consists of twenty-eight works dated from 1911 to 1980 from the collection of Ray Stark and his wife, Fran. The collection was donated to the museum in 2005. Two additional pieces were commissioned from Robert Irwin and Martin Puryear. After careful consideration, two sites were selected to exhibit these sculptures: the Fran and Ray Stark Sculpture Garden and the Fran and Ray Stark Sculpture Terrace. The former sits at the entrance to the museum and works as a green space where visitors can relax before walking the promenade or exploring the sculptures. Those include Henry Moore's *Bronze Form* (1986) and *Draped Reclining Mother and Baby* (1983), Isamu Noguchi's *The Tent of Holofernes* (1950) and Elisabeth Frink's *Running Man* (1978) and *Horse* (1980), all of which are carefully located to intersect harmoniously with the surrounding landscape.

The second space, the Sculpture Terrace, was conceived as a more sheltered and formally constructed area where sculptures rest on pedestals—a true open-air art gallery. This area features both figurative and abstract sculptures by Barbara Hepworth, René Magritte, Aristide Maillol, and Henry Moore.

A third group of sculptures has been installed around the museum grounds. This group includes *Standing Woman I* (1960) by Alberto Giacometti, *Figure for Landscape* (1960) by Barbara Hepworth, and *Air* (1938) by Aristide Maillol—indicated in the donation agreement as primary sculptures—as well as pieces by Ellsworth Kelly, Roy Lichtenstein, Fernand Léger, and Giacomo Manzù that were sited based on how they interact with specific architectural elements. Finally, a group of abstract and kinetic sculptures from the postwar period, including work by Robert Adams, Alexander Calder, Mark di Suvero, George Rickey, and Joel Shapiro, is exhibited in the Lower Terrace Garden.

THE FRAN AND RAY STARK SCULPTURE GARDEN AND THE CENTRAL GARDEN Getty Center, 1200 Getty Center Drive, Los Angeles, CA 90049 **INFO** (310) 440-7300; www.getty.edu **ARTISTS** Robert Adams, Alexander Calder, Mark di Suvero, Elisabeth Frink, Alberto Giacometti, Barbara Hepworth, Ellsworth Kelly, Fernand Léger, Roy Lichtenstein, René Magritte, Aristide Maillol, Giacomo Manzù, Joan Miró, Henry Moore, Isamu Noguchi, Martin Puryear, George Rickey, Joel Shapiro, Peter Shelton **SCULPTURES** 28 **LANDSCAPE DESIGN** Olin Partnership; Robert Irwin **ARCHITECTURE** Richard Meier **REFERENCES** Weschler, Lawrence, and Becky Cohen. *Robert Irwin: Getty Garden.* Los Angeles: Getty Publications, 2002; Boström, Antonia. *The Fran and Ray Stark Collection of 20th Century Sculpture at the J. Paul Getty Museum.* Los Angeles: J. Paul Getty Museum, 2008.

(top) Gustav Kraitz, **Apple**, 2005; (bottom) Juan Muñoz, **Conversation Piece V**, 2001, in the Barbro Osher Sculpture Garden

The Barbro Osher Sculpture Garden

De Young Museum, San Francisco, California

Founded in 1895 inside Golden Gate Park, an urban oasis in San Francisco, the de Young Museum was reopened in 2005 after a comprehensive renovation and expansion by Swiss architects Herzog & de Meuron and the implementation of a new landscape design by Walter Hood, who was responsible for *Eucalyptus Soliloquy* in the Cornerstone Gardens. The new museum spaces were designed to be compatible with the open spaces. This was achieved in part by creating paths that extend naturally through the park. Courtyards flank exhibit spaces and house such installations as *Faultline* by Andy Goldsworthy. There are also several gardens around the building, including the Barbro Osher Sculpture Garden and Terrace and the George and Judy Marcus Children's Garden.

Among the site-specific works the museum commissioned for spaces in and around the new building is *Three Gems,* a James Turrell skyspace located in the Barbro Osher Sculpture Garden. This is Turrell's first stupa—a dome-shaped Indian structure intended to house relics. It is built on a hilly area of the park and has grass growing over it. For *Drawn Stone,* Andy Goldsworthy took inspiration from the California landscape, creating a pathway delineated by slabs of stone (imported from Yorkshire) that surround the new building and seem to engage in dialogue with Hood's work.

The Barbro Osher Sculpture Garden contains work by Isamu Noguchi, Beverly Pepper, Bob Arneson, Louise Nevelson, and Claes Oldenburg and Coosje van Bruggen.

Architecture by Herzog & de Meuron

THE BARBRO OSHER SCULPTURE GARDEN de Young Museum, 50 Hagiwara Tea Garden Drive, San Francisco, CA 94118   **INFO** (415) 750-3600; www.deyoungmuseum.org
ARTISTS Bob Arneson, Andy Goldsworthy, Gustav Kraitz, Louise Nevelson, Juan Muñoz, Isamu Noguchi, Claes Oldenburg and Coosje van Bruggen, Beverly Pepper, Kiki Smith, James Turrell
SCULPTURES 10   **LANDSCAPE DESIGN** Walter J. Hood   **ARCHITECTURE** Herzog & de Meuron

Claes Oldenburg and Coosje van Bruggen, **Corridor Pin, Blue**, 1999

COLLECTORS' SPACES

(top) Ray Smith, **Red Army**, 1990; (bottom) Harry Bertoia, **Sonambient**, 1970

Sculpture Garden at Kentuck Knob

Chalk Hill, Pennsylvania

For thirty years, Bernardine and I. N. Hagan (makers of Hagan Ice Cream) lived at Kentuck Knob, an eighty-acre property in the mountains of Pennsylvania. After visiting friends at the Kaufmann Residence near Mill Run, Pennsylvania (better known as Fallingwater), the Hagans commissioned Frank Lloyd Wright, then eighty-six, to build their home. Construction took three years, and when it was completed in 1965, the couple moved in and remained there until I. N. Hagan fell ill.

In 1986, while visiting Fallingwater, Lord Palumbo heard that there was another Wright house for sale in the vicinity, and he purchased Kentuck Knob. A few weeks later, he and his wife, Hayat, took up residence there. Collectors of art and architecture by modern masters, the Palumbos decorated both the interior and the exterior of Kentuck Knob with work from around the world; they opened the property to the public in 1996.

The collection was brought to Kentuck Knob from another of Lord Palumbo's homes, Farnsworth House. The sculpture park is perfectly integrated into the landscaping around the house. Some of the sculptures are incorporated into the natural setting and partially visible from walking paths. Among the works on view are sculptures by Anthony Caro, *Apple Core* (1990) by Claes Oldenburg, *King and Queen* (1991) by David Nash, work by Jim Dine, *Red Army* (1991) by Ray Smith and *Room* (1992) by Andy Goldsworthy (originally installed in the park at Farnsworth House and then dismantled and rebuilt at Kentuck Knob), as well as a section of the Berlin Wall.

The Frank Lloyd Wright building

KENTUCK KNOB SCULPTURE GARDEN 723 Kentuck Road, Chalk Hill, PA 15421
INFO (724) 329-1901; www.kentuckknob.com   **ARTISTS** Carl Andre, Harry Bertoia, Scott Burton, Anthony Caro, Jim Dine, Andy Goldsworthy, Nicola Hicks, Peter Hide, Allen Jones, Phillip King, David Nash, Claes Oldenburg, Eva Reichl, George Rickey, Richard Serra, Ray Smith, Wendy Taylor, William Tucker, Michael Warren   **SCULPTURES** 30
ARCHITECTURE Frank Lloyd Wright   **REFERENCES** Hoffmann, Donald. *Frank Lloyd Wright's House on Kentuck Knob*. Pittsburgh, PA: University of Pittsburgh Press, 2000.

Arnaldo Pomodoro, **Triad**, 1975–79

DONALD M. KENDALL SCULPTURE GARDENS PepsiCo Headquarters, 700 Anderson Hill Road, Purchase, NY 10577 **INFO** (914) 253-2000; www.pepsico.com **ARTISTS** Judith Brown, Alexander Calder, William Crovello, Robert Davidson, Jean Dubuffet, Richard Erdman, Max Ernst, Alberto Giacometti, Gidon Graetz, Barbara Hepworth, Henri Laurens, Jacques Lipchitz, Seymour Lipton, Aristide Maillol, Marino Marini, Joan Miró, Henry Moore, Louise Nevelson, Isamu Noguchi, Claes Oldenburg, Arnaldo Pomodoro, Art Price, Bret Price, George Rickey, Auguste Rodin, Victor Salmones, George Segal, David Smith, Tony Smith, Kenneth Snelson, Ásmundur Sveinsson, Wendy Taylor, Peter Throssel, David Wynne **SCULPTURES** 45 **LANDSCAPE DESIGN** E. D. Stone Jr., Russell Page, Francois Goffinet. **ARCHITECTURE** Edward Durell Stone **REFERENCES** PepsiCo, Inc. *The PepsiCo Sculpture Gardens.* Purchase, NY: PepsiCo, 1982.

Donald M. Kendall Sculpture Gardens

PepsiCo Headquarters, Purchase, New York

In 1965, corporate giant PepsiCo decided to move its headquarters from Manhattan to the town of Purchase in nearby Westchester County. PepsiCo chief executive Donald M. Kendall did not simply stop at commissioning a new building for the company's offices. Instead, he came up with the then-groundbreaking concept of a workplace that would stand as a strong symbol of the company's identity and an international standard-bearer not only in its own field, but in the art world as well. This led to the identification of an art form that could be integrated with workspace, resulting in a place where architecture, landscape, and sculpture could work together as one. The PepsiCo headquarters and its Donald M. Kendall Sculpture Gardens embody those concepts with a 144-acre park with lawns, formal gardens, fountains, reflecting pools, and forty-five sculptures by well-known artists, most from the twentieth century.

The office complex, designed by architect Edward Durell Stone and opened in 1970, consists of seven linear buildings with shared facilities at their far ends. Only three stories high, they appear to be immersed in the surrounding green space and accentuate the horizontal character of the landscape. The central area is a courtyard with themed gardens that house smaller sculptures. Landscaping took place in several different stages: Edward D. Stone Jr. was responsible for initially laying out the park, with six thousand trees representing more than thirty-eight different varieties; a lake collects rainwater runoff from the buildings, and a circular path provides a view of the park and its sculptures. In 1981, Russell Page was assigned the five-year project of reorganizing the park in order to better integrate landscape and sculpture, bringing it into its current form. When he passed away in 1985, François Goffinet stepped in. Donald M. Kendall personally supervised the selection and placement of every single work of art in the park and in the smaller formal gardens.

The park is open to the public, and there is no admission charge. The artworks are arranged so that there is no need for a guide, nor is there any established route to follow. Kendall's aim was to create a space that would be accessible to employees and visitors alike and that would offer everyone an opportunity to encounter surprises while admiring various types of art, including architecture, at this open-air museum in a natural setting.

That said, it's best to start at the visitors center, which offers detailed maps, and then decide whether to follow the main path or just let curiosity lead the way in discovering the forty-five sculptures. Smaller works, including Auguste Rodin's *Eve* (1881), Henri Laurens's *Le Matin* (1944) and *Les Ondines* (1933), Aristide Maillol's *Marie* (1931), Art Price's *Birds of Welcome* (1977), Jacques Lipchitz's *Towards a New World* (1934), Henry Moore's *Reclining Figure* (1956) and *Locking Piece* (1962), Marino Marini's *Horse and Rider* (1952), Max Ernst's *Capricorn* (1964), and Seymour Lipton's *The Codex* (1961) and *The Wheel* (1965), are wisely located in the more circumscribed areas—in the formal gardens and on terraces and in fountains. The larger sculptures are in the park, which offsets their size and allows them to be seen in the context of the buildings and open spaces. Sculptures by the likes of David Wynne (*Dancer with a Bird,* 1974; *Girl with a Dolphin,* 1974; *The Dancers,* 1971; *Girl on a Horse,* 1976), David Smith (*Cube Totem Seven and Six,* 1961), Peter Throssel (*Standing Figures,* 1975), and Alberto Giacometti (*Large Standing Woman II* and *Large Standing Woman III,* 1960) play off of the architecture and seem to be looking out over the horizon. The monumental sculptures, such as Isamu Noguchi's *Energy Void* (1974), Henry Moore's *Double Oval* (1967), Alexander Calder's *Hats Off* (1969), William Crovello's *Katana* (1980), Arnaldo Pomodoro's *Il Grande Disco* and *Triad* (1965–68 and 1975–79), David Wynne's *Grizzly Bear* (1976), Ásmundur Sveinsson's *Through the Sound Barrier* (1977), Gidon Graetz's *Composition in Stainless Steel No. 1* (979) and Louise Nevelson's *Celebration #2* (1976) are fully integrated.

Alberto Giacometti's **Large Standing Woman II** and **Large Standing Woman III** (1960)

John Van Alstine, **Unda** (left) and **Chalice 2** (right), 1995

Adirondack Sacandaga River Sculpture Park

Adirondack State Park, Wells, New York

Adirondack Sacandaga River Sculpture Park is dedicated solely to the works of John Van Alstine. Set along the Sacandaga River, the artist's home studio is located in Adirondack State Park, a national park founded in 1882 to preserve the natural beauty of the northern part of New York State, one of the largest protected natural areas in the United States, along with Yellowstone, the Everglades, Glacier National Park, and Grand Canyon National Park.

The artist who chose to make this fascinating natural landscape his base conceives of his work on a large scale as "the union of stone and metal...the marriage of the natural with the human-made." He creates work that combines stone—a timeless natural element—with other found items from twentieth-century industrial buildings. The surrounding landscape is also part of the creative process. It serves not only as a backdrop, but as an element in the compositions that contributes to their final form.

The sculpture park sits on an old industrial woodworking site where the works have been installed by the artist himself to interface fully with natural elements. Van Alstine acquired the property in 1987 and has rebuilt it completely. On-site he has a studio with an indoor gallery and outdoor space for exhibiting larger works. The artist's work can also be found in nationally and internationally prominent collections, such as that of the Hirshhorn Museum Sculpture Garden in Washington, DC; the deCordova Sculpture Park and Museum outside Boston; Grounds for Sculpture in Hamilton, New Jersey; the Phoenix Museum Sculpture Garden; the garden of the Gulbenkian Foundation Collection in Lisbon; and the Beijing Olympic Park.

John Van Alstine, **Statio**, 2005

ADIRONDACK SACANDAGA RIVER SCULPTURE PARK Adirondack State Park,1293 Highway 30, Wells, NY 12190
INFO (518) 924-9204; www.johnvanalstine.com/docs/garden.html

163

Lake with Allen Bertoldi's **Wood Duck**, 1979

Nassau County Museum of Art Sculpture Park

Roslyn Harbor, New York

With more than forty sculptures in formal gardens surrounding the main building and elsewhere in and around the property's glades, ponds, and fields, the Nassau County Museum's sculpture garden is one of the most accessible art gardens on the East Coast, open to local residents of Long Island and anyone else who wishes to visit.

The outdoor collection was founded in 1989 and arranged on the estate of Childs Frick (son of industrialist, philanthropist, and art collector Henry Clay Frick, whose mansion on Fifth Avenue in New York City houses the Frick Collection, one of the world's most famous art museums). Upon Frick's death in 1965, the property was deeded to Nassau County and made into a museum. The main building is a three-story Georgian house from the Gilded Age of the late nineteenth century. It was named in honor of Arnold and Joan Saltzman and houses temporary exhibits as well as a permanent collection.

The surrounding land includes formal gardens commissioned by Frick's wife, Frances Dixon Frick, in 1925 and recently restored to reflect landscape architect Marian Cruger Coffin's original design. The numerous fields and paths are home to more than forty mostly large-scale sculptures dating from 1913 to 2006. Sculptures are either owned by the museum, on loan, or donated by artists or other museums and galleries. Near the house are smaller works by artists such as Jim Dine, George Rickey, Tom Otterness, Fernando Botero, and William Tucker. Other sculptures interact with natural elements and play with concepts of sequence and visual transformation. These include Allen Bertoldi's *Wood Duck* (1979), spectacularly located in the lake in front of the museum, and *Redbank 31-Nassau Variation* (1978), a site-specific piece consisting of windows that frame the landscape. Also on view are Richard Serra's *Equal Elevations Plumb Run* (1983), in a large field, and *Eraser* (1983) by Richard Nonas, which employs a few linear elements to mark the landscape.

Richard Nonas, **Eraser**, 1983

NASSAU COUNTY MUSEUM OF ART SCULPTURE PARK 1 Museum Drive, Roslyn Harbor, NY 11576
INFO (516) 484-9338; www.nassaumuseum.com **ARTISTS** Charles Arnoldi, Allen Bertoldi, Fernando Botero, Alexander Calder, Charles Cary Rumsey, Alejandro Colunga, Xavier Corbero, Jim Dine, Mark di Suvero, Adolph Gottlieb, Chaim Gross, Ana Mercedes Hoyos, Richard Hunt, William King, Bruno Lucchesi, Masayuki Nagare, Reuben Nakian, Richard Nonas, Tom Otterness, Peter Reginato, George Rickey, Niki de Saint Phalle, Richard Serra, William Tucker, Boaz Vaadia, Manolo Valdés, Max Yawney, Elyn Zimmerman **SCULPTURES** 40

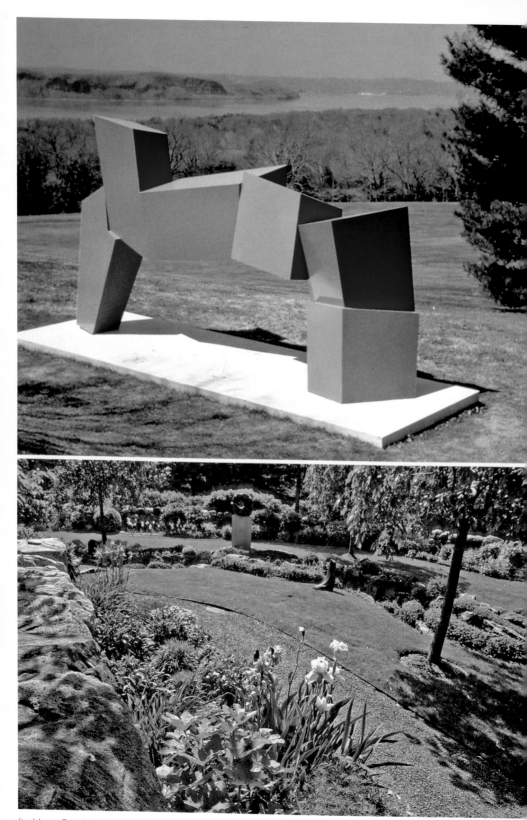

(top) James Rosati, **Lippicott II**, 1966–69; (bottom) The gardens at Kykuit

Kykuit Gardens

The Rockefeller Estate, Tarrytown, New York

Kykuit, home to John D. Rockefeller Sr. and his family, dates from the early twentieth century. It's a spectacular Georgian-style estate on the eastern shore of the Hudson River in upstate New York.

The grounds at Kykuit include formal and thematic gardens, terraces, fountains, pavilions (which Rockefeller himself designed with the assistance of landscape architect William Welles Bosworth), and a top-notch collection of exemplary artwork from 1906 to 1913.

Nelson Rockefeller (grandson of John D. Rockefeller Sr., governor of New York State, and vice-president of the United States under Gerald Ford) was a sculpture enthusiast and art collector. He was in contact with eminent figures in the New York museum and culture scene, such as Alfred H. Barr Jr., the first director of the Museum of Modern Art in New York City, and Dorothy Miller, first curator of its painting department. From 1935 to 1970, Rockefeller built his collection, which consisted of approximately 120 works by twentieth-century artists such as Aristide Maillol, Alexander Calder, Henry Moore, Pablo Picasso, Isamu Noguchi, Clement Meadmore, and Elie Nadelman. Rockefeller personally chose their locations in the Kykuit gardens.

The portion of Kykuit that belonged to Nelson Rockefeller is now the property of the National Trust for Historic Preservation and is managed and supported by the Rockefeller Brothers Fund. After renovation it opened as a museum in 1995.

The gardens around the house draw on classical traditions. They are formal and shelter the buildings. The porticoes and terraces are the perfect setting for the smaller sculptures, which include Constantin Brancusi's *Grand Oiseau* (1923) and Alberto Giacometti's *Walking Woman* (1932–33/36). The sculptures are arranged to follow the layout of the gardens with respect to vanishing points, axes, and size. Sculptures are located at the main ends of the gardens (Henry Moore's *Knife Edge, Two Piece* [1962–65]), the reflecting pools (Henry Moore's *Nuclear Energy* [1964–66]), and topiary. Farther from the buildings, the surrounding natural landscape opens up. Larger works are located here; these include Louise Nelvelson's *Atmosphere and Environment* (1967), Shinkichi Tajiri's *Granny's Knot* (1967–68) and Alexander Calder's *Large Spiny* (1966).

KYKUIT GARDENS The Rockefeller Estate, ticket office at 381 North Broadway, Sleepy Hollow, NY 10591
INFO (914) 631-8200; www.hudsonvalley.org   **ARTISTS** Robert Adams, Karel Appel, Jean Arp, Mirko Basaldella, Max Bill, Karl Bitter, Constantin Brancusi, Reg Butler, Alexander Calder, Mary Callery, Peter Chinni, Benni Efrat, Sorel Etrog, Herbert Ferber, Richard Fleischner, Lucio Fontana, Alberto Giacometti, Jean Ipoustéguy, George Kolbe, Gaston Lachaise, Alexander Liberman, Jacques Lipchitz, Aristide Maillol, Gerhard Marcks, Marino Marini, Umberto Mastroianni, Clement Meadmore, Henry Moore, Elie Nadelman, Masayuki Nagare, Louise Nevelson, Isamu Noguchi, Ezra Orion, Eduardo Paolozzi, Pablo Picasso, Arnaldo Pomodoro, Giò Pomodoro, Bernard Reder, James Rosati, Frederick Roth, David Smith, Tony Smith, Kenneth Snelson, Shinkichi Tajiri, Francois Tonetti, Fritz Wotruba   **SCULPTURES** 70
REFERENCES Pierson, Mary Louise. *The Rockefeller Family Home, Kykuit.* New York: Abbeville Press, 1998.

Serge Spitzer, **Still Life**, 2008

The Cornish Family Sculpture Garden

Aldrich Museum of Contemporary Art, Ridgefield, Connecticut

The Cornish Family Sculpture Garden is an exhibit space for the Aldrich Contemporary Art Museum. It is located next to the museum and hosts a rotating series of yearlong exhibits by contemporary artists.

The garden is an integral part of the museum, which was founded in its current location in 1964 by Larry Aldrich to house his private collection—one of the first in the United States to consist wholly of contemporary art. In 1967 the name was changed from the Larry Aldrich Museum to its current name, and a board of trustees was formed that included Larry Aldrich, Alfred H. Barr Jr., Joseph Hirshhorn, and Philip Johnson.

The museum is located in Larry Aldrich's small home town of Ridgefield, Connecticut. The Old Hundred building, as it is known, dates back to the eighteenth century. Because of the size of its rooms and the height of its ceilings, it was considered particularly suitable to house a contemporary art collection. Larry Aldrich planned from the start for the garden to exhibit sculpture year-round.

In 1981, in accordance with the founder's wishes, the permanent collection was sold so that the museum could focus entirely on emerging contemporary artists, whose work was to be displayed in temporary exhibits. In 2001 expansion was begun on the garden; that work was completed in 2004 and included the addition of the Cornish Family Sculpture Garden.

Artists with work in the garden include Arman, Bill Barrett, Robert Bart, James Buchman, Kenneth Capps, Karen Finley, Robert Grosvenor, Oded Halahmy, Duayne Hatchett, Sol LeWitt, Robert Morris, Forrest Myers, Robert Perless, Arnaldo Pomodoro, Richard Shore, Tony Smith, Serge Spitzer, Michael Somoroff, David von Schleggel, Anselm Kiefer, and Edward Tufte (known for his research on information design, as well as his work as a sculptor, which is on display at his farm in Connecticut). A 2012 exhibit displayed works commissioned by the Socrates Sculpture Park in Queens, New York, as part of its Emerging Artist Fellowship program for 2011.

Michael Somoroff, **Illumination**, 2007

THE CORNISH FAMILY SCULPTURE GARDEN Aldrich Museum of Contemporary Art, 258 Main Street, Ridgefield, CT 06877 **INFO** (203) 438-4519; www.aldrichart.org **ROTATING ARTISTS**

Steve Tobin, **Syntax**, 2006

Kouros Gallery Sculpture Garden

Ridgefield, Connecticut

The Kouros Gallery, a Manhattan art gallery opened in 1981, focuses on contemporary art, including painting, sculpture, and photography. It exhibits the work of both well-known and emerging artists. The owners, collectors Angelos and Charlotte Camillos, have a special affection for sculpture that inspired them to open the Kouros Sculpture Center, a little more than a one-hour drive from Manhattan. In a beautiful part of southern Connecticut, this park (adjacent to the owners' home) evocatively marries the natural environment and art.

The landscape at the foot of the Berkshire hills is idyllic. The road that leads to the park is long and winding, and visitors are treated to a view of environmental sculptures set on the green lawn even as they drive up the road. These include Johann Feilacher's *Untitled* (1994) at the entrance to the most private and sheltered area of the park. The well-designed house, built to the specifications of the Camillos, reflects their desire to connect with the surrounding area, creating moments of interaction and dialogue between interior and the exterior. The porticoes, walls of windows, and passageways between the house and the garden open up to offer views of works of environmental scale set in the distance in the park or around the wooded border of the property. Smaller sculptures are located in the portico and formal garden areas. The effect is one of visual and spatial relationships of varying size and intensity.

The sculpture collection represents a wide array of vocabularies and materials and includes work by artists such as Bill Barrett, Bruce Beasley, Lin Emery, Dimitri Hadzi, Don Porcaro, and Bruno Romeda.

KOUROS GALLERY SCULPTURE GARDEN 150 Mopus Bridge Road, Ridgefield, CT 06877
INFO (203) 438-7636; www.kourosgallery.com   **ARTISTS** Alexandra Athanassiades, Bill Barrett, Bruce Beasley, Zigi Ben-Haim, Emilie Benes Brzezinski, Roger Berry, Miriam Bloom, Juan Bordes, Daniel James Burt, Kris Cox, Linda Cunningham, Emanuele De Reggi, Tom Doyle, Lin Emery, Lawrence Fane, Johann Feilacher, Cristos Gianakos, Mark Hadjipateras, Maria Hall, Dimitri Hadzi, Richard Heinrich, Zero Higashida, Niki Ketchman, Ron Mehlman, Mark Mennin, Laurence Metzler, Reuben Nakian, Minoru Niizuma, Anthony Padovano, Manolis Paraschos, Marsha Pels, Vincent Péraro, Joel Perlman, Don Porcaro, Bruno Romeda, James Schmidt, Robert Sindorf, Barbara Sorensen, Nancy Steinson, Steve Tobin, Hans Van de Bovenkamp, Nicolas Vlavianos, John von Bergen, Martha Walker, Gabriel Warren, Marianne Weil, Stephen Whisler, Roger Williams **SCULPTURES 70**

The Noguchi Museum Sculpture Garden

The Noguchi Museum Sculpture Garden

Long Island City, New York

The Noguchi Museum is dedicated to the work of artist Isamu Noguchi and houses a complete collection of his works, including sculptures, designs for public spaces, gardens, and lamps—the famous Akari Light Sculptures that are still made by hand in the workshop next to the museum.

The late Noguchi himself came up with the idea for the sculpture garden and had it built in a converted industrial building next to his studio in Long Island City, Queens, New York, where he began working in the 1960s. The museum opened to the public in 1985 and was reopened after renovations in 2004 with new spaces for research (the museum partners with the Isamu Noguchi Foundation in Japan) and for the public. A second round of renovations (the museum reopened in November 2008) was intended to improve the experience for the public, as the number of visitors to the museum continued to grow. As the museum's name implies, it is a sculpture garden. The intersection of open spaces and indoor galleries forms the perfect backdrop for exhibiting work. The actual garden area is a sheltered green space with a path that runs between the works exhibited outdoors, leading to a building with ten galleries that contain sculptures, models, and drawings. The museum can also be reached from Manhattan via a tramway to Roosevelt Island that offers panoramic views; this is how the artist traveled to his studio from his home every day.

THE NOGUCHI MUSEUM SCULPTURE GARDEN 9-01 33rd Road, Long Island City, NY 11106
INFO (718) 204-7088; www.noguchi.org   **ARTISTS** Isamu Noguchi   **SCULPTURES** 300
REFERENCES Noguchi, Isamu. *The Isamu Noguchi Garden Museum.* New York: Abrams, 1999.

The Noguchi Museum Sculpture Garden

(top) Joseph Wheelwright, **Listening Stone**, 1995; (below) Ilan Averbuch, **Skirts and Pants (after Duchamp)**, 2000

DeCordova Sculpture Park and Museum

Lincoln, Massachusetts

The deCordova Sculpture Park is one of the largest sculpture parks in New England and the region's only permanent sculpture park. It offers a wide variety of routes and spaces dedicated to sculptures by American artists, which are displayed in the area surrounding the museum building.

Art enthusiast Julian de Cordova founded the museum in the 1950s in his home. In 1989 the name changed from the deCordova and Dana Museum to the deCordova Sculpture Park and Museum, partially in acknowledgement of the expanding role of the outdoor galleries, thirty-five acres of land made into a sculpture park.

The campus (as it is known) houses approximately eighty large pieces in rotation. These are broken down into three groups. The permanent collection includes work by internationally recognized artists, including George Rickey's *Three Lines* (1964), Alexander Liberman's *Cardinal Points* (1965), Beverly Pepper's *Silent Presence* (1982), John Raimondi's *Lupus* (1985), David Stronmeyer's *Campfire Girls* (1976), Hugh Townley's *Group of Three, the Pembroke Piece* (1969), Lila Katzen's *X Notion Like an H* (1978), Jonathan Bonner's *Skimmer* (1989), and Ed Shay's *Acadian Gyro* (1987).

The second group includes large sculptures on loan from private and public collections, an exchange of a dozen or so sculptures each year: previous works on display have included Mark di Suvero's *Sunflowers for Vincent* (1978–83), an homage to Vincent van Gogh, and Sol LeWitt's geometric piece *3-Pointed Star, 4-Pointed Star, 6-Pointed Star, 9-Pointed Star* (1989).

The third group consists of site-specific environmental work chosen by the museum's curators and installed in outdoor spaces for periods ranging from one to five years: past works have included *Butterfly Effect* (2004) by Rick Brown, which references the idea of transformation over time as the work changes through its contact with nature; Kathleen Driscoll's waterfall sculpture *Wall of Ice III* (1998); and plant work in progress *Bannister Trees* (1990) by Daniel Ladd.

In 2012, the ecological installation *Endangered Trees of New England* by artist Alan Sonfist was installed. Sonfist is best known for his *Time Landscape* (1978) in Manhattan. In *Endangered Trees* he reproduced the leaves of four types of endangered plants and buried a time capsule containing the seeds of each tree under each sculpture.

The expansion plan for the park was made possible by Paul Master-Karnik, director of the museum since 1984, who oversaw the expansion and renovation. One section of the park, Alice's Garden, is dedicated each year to a one-person show by an individual American artist. This garden was designed with landscape artist studio Pellettieri Associates and opened in 2000.

DECORDOVA SCULPTURE PARK AND MUSEUM 51 Sandy Pond Road, Lincoln, MA 01773
INFO (781) 259-8355; www.decordova.org   **ARTISTS** Ilan Averbuch, David Berry, Caroline Bowne Court Blessing, Jonathan Bonner, Bill Botzow, Dove Bradshaw, Rick Brown, John Buck, Cosimo Cavallaro, Tim de Christopher, Leila Daw, Dorothy Dehner, Michael Dennis, Jim Dine, Mark di Suvero, Carlos Dorrien, Kathleen Driscoll, Alfred Duca, Rico Eastman, Lars-Erik Fisk, Christopher Frost, Charles Ginnever, George Greenamyer, William Harby, Bryan Hunt, Lila Katzen, Dennis Kowal, Daniel Ladd, Sol LeWitt, Alexander Liberman, Robert Lobe, Paul Matisse, Mark Mennin, Reuben Nakian, Eric Nelson, Isamu Noguchi, Elliot Offner, Albert Paley, Beverly Pepper, Marianna Pineda, John Raimondi, George Rickey, Richard Rosenblum, Wendy Ross, John Ruppert, Ron Rudnicki, Robert Schelling, Ed Shay, Tommy Simpson, Dean Snyder, Alan Sonfist, Jane South, David Stromeyer, Margaret Swan, Hugh Townley, John Van Alstine, Ursula von Rydingsvard, Paul Voss, Kitty Wales, Joseph Wheelwright, John Wilson   **SCULPTURES** 80   **REFERENCES** Capasso, Nick, and deCordova Museum and Sculpture Park. *DeCordova Sculpture Park Guide*. Lincoln, MA: DeCordova, 1997.

Alan Sonfist, **Endangered Trees of New England: Sugar Maple, Burr Oak, American Chestnut, American Elm**, 2012

Alexander Liberman, **Abracadabra**, 1992

Pyramid Hill Sculpture Park

Hamilton, Ohio

Sitting on three hundred acres of land on the banks of the Great Miami River in southern Ohio, Pyramid Hill was created to preserve the environment in one of the most lush and rich natural regions in the United States. For this reason, public use, mostly by residents of the area, was a major concern. The park was designed to feature sporting and recreational facilities, while the landscape and character of the site were kept equally in mind. Programs are held that encourage direct interaction with nature, and sculpture plays a key role, accompanying viewers as they discover the park and learn about art, botany, geology, and horticulture.

The name Pyramid Hill was taken from the first piece that founder Harry Wilks commissioned in the 1980s for the forty acres of land that would eventually be turned into the park: his home, Pyramid House, an underground residence built into a hill. The only visible part of the house is a glass pyramid that sits atop the main room. Surrounding lands were acquired and over time this became Pyramid Hill Sculpture Park, which today has its own foundation.

Wilks built the original collection around the concept of art and nature. About fifty large sculptures are scattered along the natural paths, displayed on hilly terrain consisting of fields, six artificial lakes, and wooded areas with numerous species of trees, including oak, maple, ash, and beech. Alexander Liberman's polyhedral *Abracadabra* (1992) reflects these features and has become the park's signature piece. The park opened in 1996 with three sculptures, but the collection has expanded since then to include work by Jon Isherwood, Clement Meadmore, Bill Barrett, George Sugarman, and Tony Rosenthal, to name just a few. A collection of ancient sculptures was added in 2009 and is exhibited in the indoor galleries.

PYRAMID HILL SCULPTURE PARK 1763 Hamilton-Cleves Road, State Route 128, Hamilton, OH 45013 **INFO** (513) 868-1234; www.pyramidhill.org **ARTISTS** John Adduci, Jim Agard, Bill Barrett, Ed Benavente, Harold Betz, Carl Billingsley, Walter Driesbach, Michael Dunbar, Josefa Filkosky, Martin Gantman, Tom Gibbs, Harry Gordon, John Hock, Jon Isherwood, Greg John, Dan Kainz, Jim Killy, Alexander Liberman, Sam McKinney, Clement Meadmore, Ann Melanie, Brian Monaghan, John Parker, Joel Perlman, Michael Poast, Tony Rosenthal, Obie Simonis, Christoph Spath, George Sugarman, Michael Tearney, Stan Thomson, Barry Tinsley, Joseph Wheelright, Ken Valimaki, Clasina Van Bemmel **SCULPTURES** 50

Jonathan Borofsky, **Man with Briefcase**, 1987

General Mills Sculpture Garden

General Mills Headquarters, Minneapolis, Minnesota

The General Mills Sculpture Garden was created in the 1980s as a natural extension of the company's impressive art collection. Initially, the pieces in this collection were largely displayed in offices and other indoor areas. An additional sixteen sculptures by contemporary artists were installed on the terraces, in the courtyards, and in the gardens of the eighty-five acres of company land surrounding the headquarters (designed by Skidmore, Owings & Merrill in 1958 and located just a few minutes away from the Walker Art Center). The landscaping was handled by William A. Rutherford, the landscape architect behind the Storm King Art Center, who tends to employ a naturalistic approach.

In 2002, after General Mills was reorganized and new buildings and other facilities were added—in response to the growing number of employees—the outdoor spaces needed to be revisited as well. Landscape architects Thomas Oslund and Tadd Kreun of Oslund and Associates handled the new landscape project. Sculptures from the collection were moved and reinstalled according to the new design. The poetic and idyllic landscape of lawns, a canal that runs between the buildings and spills into a small lake, and two planted courtyards were all used to create this restful and relaxing oasis of approximately thirty-five acres.

The park is dominated by the enormous Jonathan Borofsky sculpture *Man with Briefcase* (1987), which is cut out of a sheet of steel several centimeters thick and casts an ironic eye at corporate culture. *Stone Court* (1988) by Jackie Ferrara is also monumental and consists of a wall dug into the side of a hill. It has become a place for employees to relax and a site for company events. The artist Siah Armajani was commissioned by the company to create a covered walkway that protects the parking area in winter and creates various light effects by day and by night.

Other artists whose work is shown in the outdoor spaces include Richard Serra, Mel Kendrick, and Richard Artschwager.

GENERAL MILLS SCULPTURE GARDEN 726 Vineland Place, Minneapolis, MN 55403 **INFO** (612) 230-6400; www.genmills.com **ARTISTS** Siah Armajani, Richard Artschwager, Steve Beyer, Andrea Blum, Jonathan Borofsky, Scott Burton, Pietro Consagra, Jackie Ferrara, Richard Fleischner, Jene Highstein, Mel Kendrick, Philip Larson, John Newman, Richard Serra, Elyn Zimmerman **SCULPTURES** 16 **LANDSCAPE DESIGN** Oslund and Associates (original design by William A. Rutherford) **ARCHITECTURE** Skidmore, Owings & Merrill

General Mills Sculpture Garden

Won H. Lee, **The Meditators**, 2004

The Benini Studio and Sculpture Ranch

Johnson City, Texas

The Benini Foundation transformed 125 acres of land in Texas Hill Country into a show-case for contemporary artists. The foundation was created in Florida in 1978 to serve as the studio of Benini, an Italian artist. From there it moved to Texas to the former site of President Lyndon B. Johnson's Deer Ranch. The buildings that were added now house an art library and a gallery where work from the artist's forty-year career is exhibited.

The surrounding park is known as the Sculpture Ranch. The name helps define the nature of this open space and the role that the Texan countryside plays in ground-ing the works installed there, beginning with the figurative sculpture of a bull *Paladin* (2008) by Bettye Hamblen Turner, which greets visitors at the entrance. The artists come from various backgrounds, but most of them are local. The works are all for sale, with the exception of those acquired by the owners for their permanent collection. The main requirement is that the sculptures be large enough to stand out in the vast Texan landscape, and that they be solid enough to handle the atmosphere and climate, which have ruined several sculptures in the past. Each piece is exhibited for a minimum of two years. The ranch is open to visitors, artists, and collectors year-round and encourages guided tours.

Jerry Daniel, **The Dancers**, 2000

THE BENINI STUDIO AND SCULPTURE RANCH 377 Shiloh Road, Johnson City, TX 78636
INFO (830) 868-2247; www.benini.com **ARTISTS** Benini, Joseph Buchanan, Marshall Cunningham, Rick Cunningham, Jerry Daniel, Pete Deise, Tom Edwards, Kristin H. Eyfells, Bob Fowler, Jack Gron, Robert Hamric, Zena Stetka Howe, Loren Impson, Randy Jewart, Jim La Paso, Won H. Lee, Peter Mangan, Bryan Massey, Robert McConaughy, Gualtiero Mocenni, Pat Musick, Arny Nadler, Nic Noblique, Michelle O'Michael, Terry Rowlett, Sam Spiczka, Russ Thayer, Bettye Hamblen Turner, Zaro **SCULPTURES** 100

Pete Deise, **Ascension**, 2006

(top) Donald Judd, **100 untitled works in mill aluminum**, detail, 1982–86;
(bottom) Claes Oldenburg and Coosje van Bruggen, **Monument to the Last Horse**, 1991. Photograph by Attilio Maranzano

Chinati Foundation

Marfa, Texas

A visit to the Chinati Foundation is one of the most intense aesthetic experiences available. As Peter Flückiger writes in his book *Architecture in Marfa*: "Donald Judd is best known as a sculptor—though he rejected that term—but what Marfa illuminates are his talents in other areas such as architecture, landscape design, furniture. The Artillery Sheds, the aluminum and concrete boxes, the cottonwood trees and the rows of buildings are all part of a creation by Judd. Nothing is by accident."

Conceived and created by Donald Judd (1928–94) on a former military base, the Chinati Foundation was designed to preserve and present to the public large-scale sculptures by a limited number of artists dealing with the theme of the relationships among art, architecture, and landscape. Construction of the museum started in 1979 with support from the Dia Art Foundation in New York and ended in 1986, when the museum was opened to the public as a nonprofit independent institution. Initially, it exhibited work by Donald Judd, John Chamberlain, and Dan Flavin. Over the years the collection grew to include, among others, fifteen concrete outdoor sculptures by Judd (installed over almost a mile of land along the north-south axis of the foundation); one hundred of Judd's aluminum sculptures in the galleries; twenty-five sculptures by John Chamberlain; and an installation by Dan Flavin in six former barracks restructured by Judd and used as exhibit space. Each artist's work is located in a separate dedicated area. *Monument to the Last Horse* (1991) by Claes Oldenburg and Coosje van Bruggen was donated by the artists, longtime friends of Judd, and marks the burial place of the last cavalry horse for the military installation that once sat on the land.

The Chinati Foundation works with the Judd Foundation, created in 1996 after the artist's death, for the purpose of making his work available to the public in accordance with his will.

This is just one of the places in Marfa where Donald Judd's work and collection can be viewed. Among the others is La Mansana de Chinati/The Block, the artist's home. During the annual open house, the foundation's buildings are open to the public and have exhibited work by John Chamberlain, Claes Oldenburg and Coosje van Bruggens, Larry Bell, and Yayoi Kusama, as well as vintage design pieces (Gerrit Rietveld, Alvar Aalto, Ludwig Mies van der Rohe) collected by Judd.

CHINATI FOUNDATION 1 Cavalry Row, Marfa, TX 79843   **INFO** (432) 729-4362; www.chinati.org
ARTISTS Alvar Aalto, Carl Andre, Ingólfur Arnarsson, Larry Bell, John Chamberlain, Dan Flavin, Roni Horn, Donald Judd, Ilya Kabakov, Yayoi Kusama, Richard Long, Ludwig Mies van der Rohe, Claes Oldenburg and Coosje van Bruggen, David Rabinowitch, Gerrit Rietveld, John Wesley   **SCULPTURES** 150   **REFERENCES** Flückiger, Urs Peter, and Donald Judd. *Donald Judd: Architecture in Marfa, Texas.* Basel: Birkhäuser, 2007.

Donald Judd, **15 untitled works in concrete**, detail, 1980−84

Ann Hamilton, **tower**·**Oliver Ranch**, 2003–07

Oliver Ranch Foundation Sculpture Collection

Geyserville, California

Collector Steven Oliver lives with his wife, Nancy, on Geyserville Ranch in Sonoma County, the location of the Oliver Ranch Foundation Sculpture Collection.

This sculpture collection began with the 1985 acquisition of Judith Shea's *Shepherd's Muse* (1985–88). The Olivers wanted to create a collection of art in its purest form, where each work is designed in response to a place and cannot be moved or sold. The process of creating the park is a work in progress that has not, over the last twenty-five years, followed any particular plan or established rules. Instead, it allows artists significant decision-making power without the pressure usually imposed upon them by work on commission for public display.

The only rule is that artists are asked to visit the ranch at least three times at different times of the year before submitting a proposal, in order to create work that will mesh with the landscape; there is no time limit for creating the sculptures, which are commissioned one at a time. (Until 1994, there were two pieces commissioned per year, but over time the Olivers became unconcerned with the length of time required to create the sculptures and instead began to concentrate on the process of creating them.) Some of the sculptures are designed and created on site, while others are simply assembled at the ranch. The only ephemeral environmental work is by Andy Goldsworthy, who created six temporary pieces in 1992 that are still partly visible. The eighteen installations in the park include *Untitled* (1998–99) by Bruce Nauman, a staircase with 289 steps of varying sizes (depending on the shape of the underlying landscape) that connects the entrance to the ranch with the owners' house. The collection also includes work by Richard Serra, *Snake Eyes and Boxcars* (1990–93); Terry Allen; and Miroslaw Balka (the only outdoor sculpture by this artist in the United States, the piece reconstructs the foundation of the house in Poland where he was born in an evocative play on memory and loss). Also represented are Roger Berry, Ellen Driscoll, Bill Fontana, Kristin Jones, Andrew Ginzel, Dennis Leon, Jim Melchert, Martin Puryear, David Rabinowitch, Jim Jennings, Fred Sandback, Judith Shea, Robert Stackhouse, and Ursula von Rydingsvard. The latest installation is Ann Hamilton's *tower • Oliver Ranch* (2003–07), which resembles a silo or other type of farm building and is used as a performance space.

OLIVER RANCH FOUNDATION SCULPTURE COLLECTION 22205 River Road, Geyserville, CA 95441 **INFO** (707) 857-3975; www.oliverranchfoundation.org   **ARTISTS** Terry Allen, Miroslaw Balka, Roger Barry, Ellen Driscoll, Bill Fontana, Andrew Ginzel, Andy Goldsworthy, Ann Hamilton, Jim Jennings, Kristin Jones, Dennis Leon, Jim Melchert, Bruce Nauman, Martin Puryear, David Rabinowitch, Fred Sandback, Richard Serra, Judith Shea, Robert Stackhouse, Ursula von Rydingsvard   **SCULPTURES** 20   **REFERENCES** Brookman, Donna. "Collecting Experience: A Conversation with Steven Oliver." *Sculpture* 21, no. 8 (October 2002).

Miroslaw Balka, **43 × 30 × 2, 43 × 30 × 2, 1554 × 688 × 10**, 1995–96

MAPS

NORTHEAST

MIDWEST

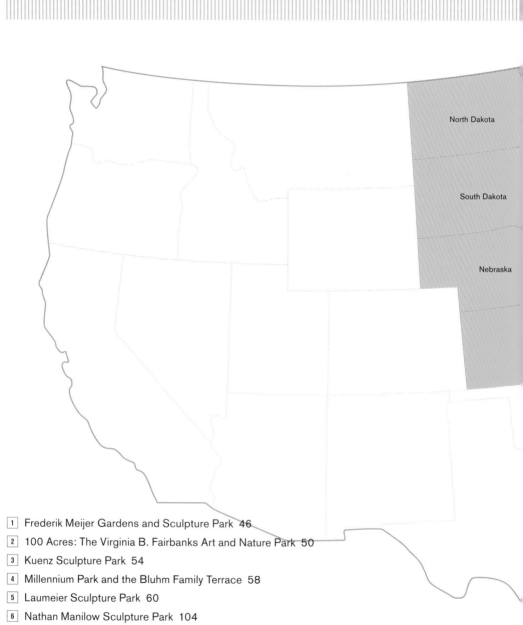

North Dakota

South Dakota

Nebraska

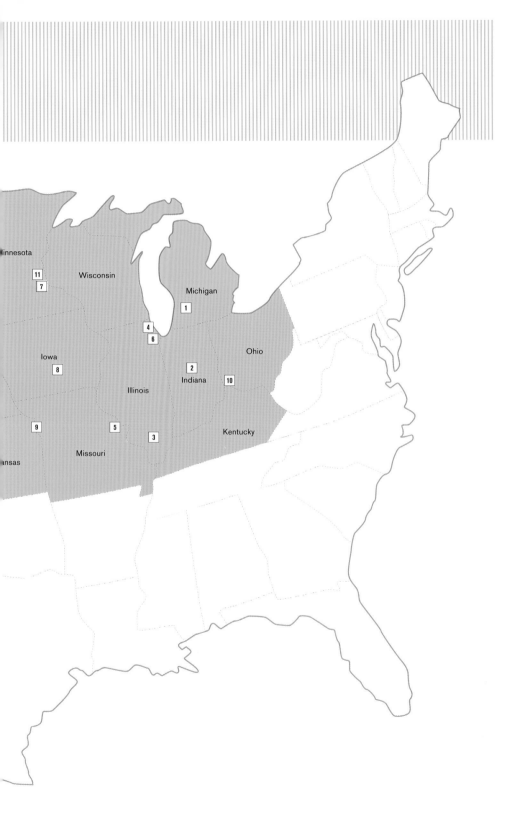

SOUTH/SOUTHWEST

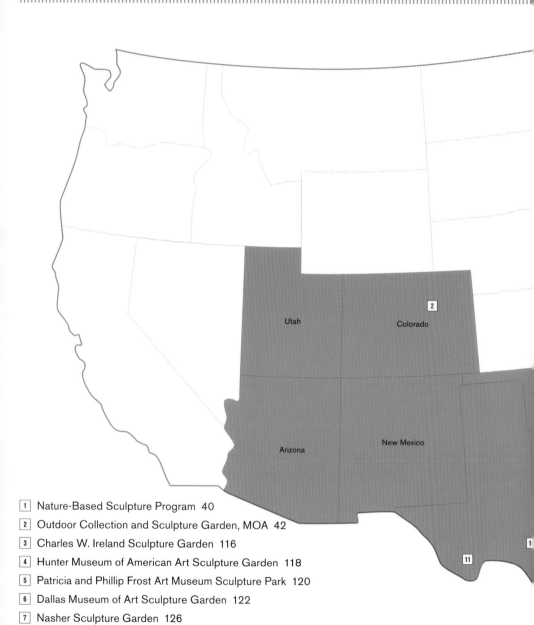

Utah

Colorado

2

Arizona

New Mexico

11

WEST

ADDITIONAL PARKS

California

LA JOLLA
Stuart Collection at the University of California, San Diego
The Stuart Collection was created in 1982, based on an agreement between the university and the Stuart Foundation to transform the University of California, San Diego campus into a sculpture park with works on commission. The campus is located on a plateau with a striking view of the ocean. It incorporates various public spaces, plazas, and gardens. Works include *Trees* (1986) by Terry Allen, a sound installation in which each member of a group of eucalyptus trees is given its own sound. Also working with plant materials (eucalyptus trees), in 1983 Robert Irwin created *Two Running Violet V Forms*, an installation formed by a geometric grid of trees with a violet plastic structure running between them. Positioned above the walkway, it reflects changes in light and color from the surrounding environment, playing with perception of natural elements. Jackie Ferrara, who has been creating architectural spaces and structures since the 1960s, worked on the public space *Terrace* (1991), developed with a team of architects (Moore Ruble Yudell) and a landscape designer (Andrew Spurlock). *Unda* (1987) by Ian Hamilton Finlay is an installation composed of five blocks; the word *unda* (Latin for "wave") is engraved and repeated on each block, and the surface imitates an ocean wave—a metaphor for the speed and flow of language. [*Landmarks: Sculpture Commissions for the Stuart Collection at the University of California, San Diego*, Rizzoli, 2001] *(858) 534-2117; http://stuartcollection.ucsd.edu*

LA JOLLA / SAN DIEGO
Museum of Contemporary Art
These collections are exhibited in two locations, one in La Jolla and one in Los Angeles. Some of the sculptures are situated outside the museum, including (in the La Jolla location) *Three Cairns* (2003), the second part of an Andy Goldsworthy piece intended for multiple points around the United States. *(858) 454-3541; www.mcasd.org*

OAKLAND
Oakland Museum of Art Sculpture Garden
The Oakland Museum of Art was designed in the 1960s by Roche-Dinkeloo and Dan Kiley, who paid particular attention to the outdoor spaces—patios, terraces, and gardens—where the sculpture collection is carefully curated. *(510) 318-8400; www.museumca.org*

PASADENA
Norton Simon Museum Sculpture Garden
The gardens around this museum were created in the 1970s to exhibit the large collection of industrialist Norton Simon. The collection consists of work from the nineteenth and twentieth centuries, as well as an excellent selection of ancient Asian art. The sculptures sit amid lush vegetation designed by landscape architect Nancy Goslee Power. The museum's interior spaces were expanded in the 1990s based on a Frank Gehry design. Surrounded by 180 species of plants and various reflecting pools, this modern collection consists of approximately twenty sculptures by artists such as Auguste Rodin, Jacques Lipchitz, and Henry Moore. *(626) 449-6840; www.nortonsimon.org*

SAN DIEGO
May S. Marcy Sculpture Court and Garden at the San Diego Museum of Art
The sculpture garden annexed to the courtyard of the San Diego Museum of Art is a small outdoor space that contains works from the museum's permanent modern and contemporary sculpture collection. Created in the 1960s by a donation from the Norton Wallbridges, the space initially was the site of large-scale works from the Wallbridges' collection, including *Cubi XV* (1963), part of a series by David Smith; *Reclining Figure: Arch Leg* (1971–72) by Henry Moore; *Solar Bird* (1966) by Joan Miró; *Spinal Column* (1968) by Alexander Calder; and sculptures by Louise Nevelson, Barbara Hepworth, Masayuki Nagare, and Francisco Zúñiga acquired by the museum with funds provided by the collectors. *(619) 232-7931; www.sdmart.org*

SAN FRANCISCO
SFMOMA Sculpture Terrace
The San Francisco Museum of Modern Art opened its sculpture garden in 2009. The garden consists of two open spaces and a glass pavilion with a view of the city skyline. Pieces from the museum's collection are exhibited in rotation. *(415) 357-4000; www.sfmoma.org*

WOODSIDE
Djerassi Resident Artists Program
This foundation hosts a residency program for artists in which sculptors are invited for varying lengths of time to create work in the foundation's open spaces. Fifty sculptures are currently on exhibit, and they can be visited year-round from sunrise to sunset. *(650) 747-1250; www.djerassi.org*

Colorado

DENVER
Martin Plaza at Denver Art Museum (DAM)
The Denver Art Museum was founded in 1893 and houses a large collection of art with pieces ranging from ancient to modern. In 1971 the museum was expanded based on a design for its North Building by Gio Ponti. In 2006 the Frederic C. Hamilton Building, designed by Daniel Libeskind (his first in the United States), was added. At the same time, the museum's outdoor spaces were redesigned—most notably Martin Plaza. Developed around the new Hamilton Building, the plaza links a nearby public park to the museum and also connects the museum buildings to each other. DAM's modern and contemporary collection includes several large-scale works exhibited in this space that beg comparison with the architecture of the buildings: *Big Sweep*, part of a group of oversized household objects by Claes Oldenburg and Coosje van Bruggen, was commissioned by the museum in 1999 and placed on the southern side of the new museum wing; *Denver Monoliths* (2004–5) by Beverly Pepper is one of the largest sculptures ever commissioned for an outdoor space. *Scottish Angus Cow and Calf* (2001) by Dan Ostermiller stand out of the Hamilton Building, in Hindery Family Park. This pair was originally intended for the ranch of businessman Leo Hindery, who then donated the work to the museum with funds for its installation and upkeep. A fourth installation, *ENGI* (2006) by Tatsuo Miyajima, stands at the entrance to the Hamilton Building. It consists of about eighty mirrored disks that blink and project numbers from one through nine. *(720)865-5000; www.denverartmuseum.org*

Connecticut

GREENWICH
Brant Foundation Art Study Center
The Brant Foundation is a nonprofit facility dedicated to contemporary art and design. It began as a study center for institutions and researchers created on the property of collector and founder Peter Brant. Opened to the public in 2011, it may be visited by appointment and has a sculpture garden with work from the Brant collection. *(203)869-0611; www.brantfoundation.org*

Florida

MIAMI
Miami Art Museum
The Miami Art Museum was designed as part of Museum Park Miami and opened in 2012. The museum is housed in a green building designed by the firm Herzog & de Meuron to suit the area's climate. Indoor and outdoor spaces communicate with each other fluidly, not only for aesthetic purposes (the outside envelope of the building was made with plant material), but also for functionality; natural elements help make the building more sustainable. New site-specific installation spaces are also planned for work that will be commissioned from contemporary artists to expand the museum's collection. *(305)375-3000; www.miamiartmuseum.org*

Georgia

ATLANTA
Atlanta Botanical Garden
The city's botanical garden contains a permanent sculpture collection and also hosts traveling exhibits, including the recent show *Moore in America: The Monumental Sculpture of Henry Moore*, which had previously been exhibited at the New York Botanical Garden. *(404)876-5859; www.atlantabotanicalgarden.org*

ATLANTA
High Museum of Art
This museum, designed by Richard Meier in 1983, with three new additions by Renzo Piano Building Workshop in 2005, is surrounded by open spaces that house the collection's sculptures. Many of these have become signature pieces that represent the museum. Renzo Piano's famous plaza is home to sculptures by artists such as Roy Lichtenstein and Auguste Rodin. *(404)733-4400; www.high.org*

Illinois

EVANSTON
**Mary and Leigh Block Museum of Art
Sculpture Garden at Northwestern University**
The works in this collection dot the sculpture garden of Northwestern University (north of Chicago), which stands in front of the museum of the same name; artists represented include Joan Miró, Barbara Hepworth, Arnaldo Pomodoro, and Henry Moore. *(847)491-4000; www.blockmuseum.northwestern.edu*

SHAUMBURG
Chicago Athenaeum's International Sculpture Park
The Chicago Athenaeum is an international museum founded in 1988 and dedicated to archiving and making available materials in the field of architecture and design. The International Sculpture Park of the Chicago Athenaeum is located approximately one hour from Chicago and houses sculptures by national and international contemporary artists. *(815)777-4444; www.chi-athenaeum.org/park.htm*

SKOKIE
Skokie Northshore Sculpture Park
In the 1980s, the Metropolitan Water Reclamation District of Greater Chicago was created, and proposals were sought for designs that would reclaim land to create a public park as well as a nonprofit organization for its maintenance and enrichment through works of art. This park was created in an abandoned area between the Chicago River and McCormick Boulevard in Skokie. *(847)679-4265; www.sculpturepark.org*

SKOKIE & DES PLAINES
The two campuses of Oakton Community College, the Des Plaines Campus and the Ray Hartstein Campus, have a large open-air collection featuring works by more than one hundred area artists. *(847)635-1600; www.oakton.edu*

Indiana

COLUMBUS
Miller House and Garden at Indianapolis Museum of Art (IMA)
The IMA acquired the well-regarded Miller House and Garden in Columbus (near Indianapolis). The house is now open to the public and may be visited year-round. The Eero Saarinen–designed house is surrounded by a masterful garden by Dan Kiley, completed in 1955. *(317)923-1331; www.imamuseum.org*

Louisiana

NEW ORLEANS

The Sydney and Walda Besthoff Sculpture Garden

Reopened after a full renovation and replanting, the sculpture garden of the New Orleans Museum of Art is home to more than fifty sculptures, forty-four of which were donated to the museum by the Besthoff Foundation. Sculptures include work by Émile-Antoine Bourdelle, Louise Bourgeois, Luciano Fabro, Henry Moore, Jacques Lipchitz, Kenneth Snelson, Alison Saar, Joel Shapiro, Jean-Michel Othoniel, and Arnaldo Pomodoro. [Miranda Lash, *The Sydney and Walda Besthoff Sculpture Garden at the New Orleans Museum of Art: Art Spaces*, NOMA-Scala, 2012] *(504) 658-4100; www.noma.org*

Maryland

SOLOMONS

Annmarie Garden

Donated to Calvert County by Francis and Ann Koenig, this garden houses environmental and site-specific work. Since 2003, when it became affiliated with the Smithsonian Institution, the sculpture garden has been lent works by artists and other institutions. The garden, which surrounds a relatively recent museum building, is home largely to sculptures from the collection of the Hirshhorn Museum in Washington, DC. The garden was named in honor of Ann Marie Koenig, who, together with her husband, Francis, acquired the land on Solomons Island and established the garden. *(410) 326-4640; www.annmariegarden.org*

Massachusetts

BOSTON

Arts on the Point

Paul Tucker, a professor at the University of Massachusetts, conceived of a contemporary outdoor sculpture collection at the state university's Boston campus. The campus is adjacent to the park at Columbia Point, near the Boston harbor, and faces the ocean. Designed as an open-air *kunsthalle*, the park is home to a dozen permanent sculptures. The John F. Kennedy Presidential Library and Museum, in a 1977 I. M. Pei building, is located nearby. *(617) 287-5000; www.umb.edu/in_the_community/arts/arts_on_the_point*

SHEFFIELD

Butler Sculpture Park

This park in Sheffield Valley is home to more than sixty-five sculptures by Robert Butler. It was opened in 1991 by the artist and his wife, Susan, who spent four years preparing the land for the installation of the artwork. Pathways, lawns, and open-air rooms for displaying sculptures allow visitors to enjoy the surrounding natural environment. Smaller sculptures are located in a gallery at the entrance to the park and in two exhibit spaces near the artist's studio. *(413) 229-8924*

Michigan

BLOOMFIELD HILLS

Cranbrook Academy of Art

The Cranbrook Academy of Art, northwest of Detroit, was founded by philanthropist George Gough Booth. The campus was designed in 1928 by Finnish architect Eliel Saarinen, who served as president of the school until his death in 1950. Conceived as a true community for artists, it has hosted many high-profile figures in the worlds of international art, architecture, and design, including Ray and Charles Eames, Florence Knoll, Jack Lenor Larsen, Donald Lipski, Duane Hanson, and Hani Rashid. The campus offers an array of architectural riches, including the expanded Academy and Art Museum by Rafael Moneo and the Institute of Science by Steven Holl. Visitors can admire the academy's open-air sculpture collection, which includes numerous pieces by Carl Milles (Cranbrook's collection is the second largest of his work in the world, after the Milles Garden in Stockholm) as well as ten or so sculptures that are typically on temporary loan from other artists. Several buildings can be visited, including Saarinen's house and its attached garden, built from 1928 to 1930, which sits adjacent to the house where Carl Milles lived. The Saarinen house was conceived as a complete work of art and designed down to the last detail, from its general layout to its furnishings. *(248) 645-3300; www.cranbrookart.edu*

Minnesota

FRANCONIA

Franconia Sculpture Park

Modeled on the Socrates Sculpture Park in Queens, New York, and located outside of an urban environment, this park was founded by artist John Hock and reopened in 2006 in a new, larger location. The park exhibits work by artists who spend varying amounts of time participating in temporary residencies. *(651) 257-6668; www.franconia.org*

Missouri

ST. LOUIS

St. Louis Art Museum Blanke Sculpture Terrace and Outdoor Gardens

The garden at the St. Louis Art Museum, closed for renovation at the time of this writing, houses a permanent collection of open-air sculpture. In 2007 the museum was expanded, with the goal of increasing exhibit space, facilities, and public spaces in order to make this Forest Park institution a focal point for culture in the city. In 2008 ground was broken for the new building, designed by English architect David Chipperfield and landscape architect Michel Desvigne. Downtown St. Louis is home to many cultural institutions and is a place where architecture, art, and landscape intersect quite enjoyably. Other major institutions include the Contemporary Art Museum; the Mildred Lane Kemper Art Museum at Washington University, with a sculpture plaza designed by Fumihiko Maki; and the Pulitzer Foundation for the Arts in poetic spaces designed by Tadao Ando. The city's great urban landmark is Eero Saarinen's *Gateway Arch*. Located in the Jefferson National Expansion Memorial along the Mississippi River, it looms over a park originally designed by Dan Kiley. *(314) 721-0072; www.slam.org*

Nebraska

LINCOLN
Sheldon Memorial Art Gallery
The outdoor collection of the Sheldon Memorial Art Gallery was installed in 1970 in the sculpture garden adjacent to the Philip Johnson building of the same name. It is dedicated to Mary Frances Sheldon and her brother, Adams Bromley Sheldon, and contains thirty-five pieces by internationally recognized artists. *(402) 472-2461; www.sheldonartgallery.org*

New York

BEACON
Dia:Beacon
The Beacon location of the Dia Foundation (Riggio Galleries) is housed in a former factory complex on the banks of the Hudson River and exhibits works of minimalist and land art. The collection includes *Beacon Poin*t (2007), an environmental art installation designed by landscape artist George Trakas as part of the Long Dock Project, a plan to transform this area of the Hudson Valley, once full of warehouses and railroads, into an environmentally friendly place with eco-technological services and green public spaces. Trakas's installation is an integral part of that mission. *(845) 440-0100; www.diabeacon.org*

BUFFALO
Albright-Knox Art Gallery
This museum is known as an excellent spot to view American and European sculpture and painting from the last fifty years. Most of the work was acquired using donations from Seymour H. Knox. Sculptures are located in the courtyard (part of a 1962 addition by Gordon Bunshaft) and in the spaces surrounding the museum. *(716) 882-8700; www.albrightknox.org*

NEW YORK CITY
Wave Hill
Built in 1843, Wave Hill in the Bronx has been home to well-known figures such as Theodore Roosevelt, Mark Twain, and Arturo Toscanini. In 1965 it became a nonprofit facility dedicated to environmental education. Initially the sculpture garden featured pieces from the Hirshhorn Museum collection, but its focus later sharpened on contemporary art. At the moment, its various spaces act as stages for thematic exhibits, landscape work created on site each summer, and the work of emerging artists. *(718) 549-3200; www.wavehill.org*

PLATTSBURGH
Plattsburgh Sculpture Park at State University of New York Plattsburgh
This park is run by the SUNY Plattsburgh Museum in the Northern Adirondack/Champlain Valley area. Monumental sculptures and installations are on view year-round. *(518) 564-2474; www.plattsburgh.edu/museum*

PURCHASE
Purchase College
The campus of Purchase College-State University of New York sits across from the PepsiCo headquarters. The campus was created through the initiative of then-governor Nelson Rockefeller, who acquired the property in 1967; it was designed as a city in the country by well-known architect Edward Larrabee Barnes. The campus is also the site of the Neuberger Museum (in a building by Philip Johnson and John Burgee), which houses an open-air collection of about twenty-five sculptures scattered over the campus, including two that welcome visitors at the entrance: *Large Two Forms* (1969) by Henry Moore and the famous *East Coast Cairn* (2001), part of Andy Goldsworthy's multiple-site *Three Cairns Project*. *(914) 251-6100; www.neuberger.org*

New Mexico

QUEMADO
The Lightning Field
Walter De Maria's permanent land-art installation, created in 1977 in a remote area of the New Mexico desert, is curated by the Dia Art Foundation of New York and may be visited by appointment from May through October. *(505) 898-3335; www.diacenter.org/sites/main/lightningfield*

North Carolina

RALEIGH
North Carolina Museum of Art
This museum has been renovated and expanded, with new exhibit spaces and outdoor areas for the installation of sculptures. The outdoor spaces were designed by Peter Walker/PWP and are intended to serve as sites for large-scale and environmental work. The project also included the renovation of Museum Park, a sculpture park adjacent to the museum created in 2000, which houses a collection and is also open to the public. The initial design for an environmental park was created in 1988 as part of a plan titled The Imperfect Utopia: a Park for the New World, conceived by artist Barbara Kruger and architects Henry Smith-Miller and Laurie Hawkinson, as well as landscape architect Nicholas Quennel (see "D.P. Gottlieb, Planning the Museum Park at the North Carolina Museum of Art" in *Landscapes for Art: Contemporary Sculpture Parks,* ISC Press). *(919) 839-6262; www.ncartmuseum.org*

Ohio

COLUMBUS
Russell Page Sculpture Garden at Columbus Museum of Art
One of thirteen gardens designed in the United States (others include the PepsiCo Headquarters Sculpture Park and the garden of the Frick Collection in New York City) by the English landscape designer Russell Page, the garden (created in 1979 and renovated in 1992) is a formal space around a reflecting pool, shaded by lush plants and enhanced by both figurative and abstract sculptures, including work by Alexander Calder, Henry Moore, George Rickey, and Barbara Hepworth. *(614) 221-6801; www.columbusmuseum.org*

TOLEDO
Georgia and David K. Welles Sculpture Garden at the Toledo Museum of Art
Opened in 2001 on the occasion of the museum's one-hundredth anniversary, this sculpture garden houses twenty-one modern and contemporary works and connects the institution's large outdoor spaces. The Toledo Museum of Art (really more of a campus than a museum, given its size and collection of buildings) consists of the main building, an imposing 1912 structure designed in the Greek style, and its adjacent sculpture garden with the iconic *Stegosaurus* by Alexander Calder (1973); the University of Toledo Center for Sculptural Studies and Grove Place Studios; the University of Toledo Center for Visual Art, designed by Frank Gehry, which houses the university's art department and the museum library; and the Glass Pavilion, opened in 2006 to house the museum's highly regarded glass collection (more than five thousand pieces from ancient to contemporary) and designed by the equally highly regarded architectural firm SANAA. *(419) 255-8000; www.toledomuseum.org*

Pennsylvania

CHESTNUT HILL
Morris Arboretum of the University of Pennsylvania
Approximately twenty minutes outside of Philadelphia, along a bike path that connects the arboretum to downtown, the Morris Arboretum is one of the country's loveliest botanical gardens. Part of the University of Pennsylvania since 1932, it was founded by the Quaker Morris family and built in the Victorian style. *(215) 247-5777; www.business-services.upenn.edu/arboretum/visit.shtml*

JENKINTOWN
Abington Art Center Sculpture Park
This park houses permanent and ephemeral sculptures by artists invited to use natural elements and to construct dialogues with the surrounding landscape. The park's signature work is *A Reclamation Garden* by Winifred Lutz, begun in 1992. *(215) 887-4882; www.abingtonartcenter.org*

PHILADELPHIA
Philadelphia Museum of Art Sculpture Garden
The recent design for the sculpture garden at the Philadelphia Museum of Art by the Olin Partnership created a roof garden in the museum's new spaces. The new open-air galleries are arranged on multiple levels, on terraces and lawns that look out over the Schuylkill River and nearby Fairmount Park. The design for the open spaces was part of a wide-ranging renovation plan that involved all areas of the museum. The first installation planned will consist of five sculptures of different sizes by Isamu Noguchi. *www.philamuseum.org*

PHILADELPHIA
Rodin Museum
This Philadelphia museum houses the largest collection of Auguste Rodin's work outside of France. *(215) 763-8100; www.rodinmuseum.org*

South Carolina

MURRELLS INLET
Brookgreen Gardens
The Brookgreen Gardens, opened in 1932, were the first public sculpture gardens in the United States. They house an impressive collection of figurative American art inside a botanical park. In 2002 the Center for American Sculpture was annexed for a program with artists in residence. *(843) 235-6000; www.brookgreen.org*

Tennessee

NASHVILLE
Carell Woodland Sculpture Trail at Cheekwood
Cheekwood is a botanical garden set on the historic Cheek property and consists of several buildings and gardens that house collections of art and botanical specimens. Gardens that are open to the public include the Wills Perennial Garden, the Japanese Garden, the Turner Season Garden, the Herb Garden, and the Howe Wildflower Garden. Art and landscape intersect on the Carell Woodland Sculpture Trail. Opened in 1999 and dedicated to its patron, Monroe Carell, this trail is open year-round. The sculptures, numbering approximately fifteen and representing a high-quality group of American and European artists, were chosen specifically for their natural environment. They include *Untitled (In A Dream)* (1997) by Jenny Holzer; *Blue Pesher* (1997–99), a contemplative room by James Turrell; and *"The Order of the Present Is the Disorder of the Future"–Saint-Just* (1988) by Ian Hamilton Finlay. *(615) 356-8000; www.cheekwood.org*

Texas

DALLAS
Elizabeth Meadows Sculpture Garden
The garden of the Meadows Museum is located on the campus of Southern Methodist University and was created by Algur H. Meadows in honor of his wife. It houses twentieth-century sculptures and an installation by Santiago Calatrava, a wave structure made of 129 steel bars coated in bronze in a black granite pool. *(214) 768-2516; www.meadowsmuseumdallas.org*

FORT WORTH
The cultural district of Fort Worth includes some of the world's top museums, designed by some of the world's leading architects: the Amon Carter Museum by Philip Johnson; the Kimbell Art Museum by Louis Kahn; and the Modern Art Museum of Fort Worth by Tadao Ando, which has a sculpture garden and terrace. Among the works on exhibit is the monumental *Vortex* (2002) by Richard Serra. *(817) 738-9215; www.themodern.org*

Virginia

RICHMOND
Virginia Museum of Fine Arts
The E. Claiborne and Lora Robins Sculpture Garden was created as part of a renovation plan for the entire museum complex; its landscape architecture is by the Olin Partnership. *(804) 340-1400; www.vmfa.museum*

Washington

PORTLAND
Portland Art Museum Sculpture Garden
The design for this museum's outdoor spaces is by landscape architect Topher Delaney (who has an installation at the Cornerstone Gardens in Sonoma). A series of concrete, glass, and steel walls encloses the works, creating true open-air rooms. *(207) 775-6148; www.portlandmuseum.com*

Wisconsin

MILWAUKEE
Cudahy Gardens and Outdoor Sculptures at Milwaukee Art Museum (MAM)
The green spaces that surround the Milwaukee Art Museum's buildings—the War Memorial Center, designed by Eero Saarinen in 1957, and the Quadracci Pavilion, designed by Santiago Calatrava in 2001—are enhanced by sculptures from the museum's collection. The outdoor spaces also include the Cudahy Gardens, a series of plazas and formal gardens by Dan Kiley, completed in 2001. *(414) 224-3200; www.mam.org*

MILWAUKEE
Lynden Sculpture Garden
This garden is located at the former residence of Harry and Margaret Bradley, Milwaukee entrepreneurs and philanthropists. The collection includes forty-five works by internationally known artists such as Henry Moore, Barbara Hepworth, Clement Meadmore, and Alexander Archipenko. *(414) 446-8794; http://lyndensculpturegarden.org*

BIBLIOGRAPHY

Abascal, Jimena Blázquez, Valeria Varas, and Raúl Rispa. *Sculpture Parks in Europe: A Guide to Art and Nature*. Basel: Birkäuser, 2002.

Andrews, Malcolm. *Landscape and Western Art*. New York: Oxford University Press, 2000.

Beardsley, John. *Earthworks and Beyond: Contemporary Art in the Landscape*. New York: Abbeville, 2006.

Boettger, Suzaan. *Earthworks: Art and the Landscape of the Sixties*. Berkeley, CA: University of California Press, 2004.

Czerniak, Julia, and George Hargreaves. *Large Parks*. New York: Princeton Architectural Press, 2007.

Dempsey, Amy. *Destination Art*. London: Thames and Hudson, 2006.

Gooding, Mel, and William Furlong. *Artists, Land, Nature*. New York: Abrams, 2002.

Harper, Glenn, and Twylene Moyer. *Landscapes for Art: Contemporary Sculpture Parks*. Washington DC: ISC Press, 2008.

Jodidio, Philip. *Architecture Now! Landscape*. London: Taschen, 2012.

Kastner, Jeffrey, and Brian Wallis. *Land and Environmental Art*. London: Phaidon, 2010.

Lailach, Michael. *Land Art*. London: Taschen, 2007.

Lippincott, Jonathan. *Large Scale: Fabricating Sculpture in the 1960s and 1970s*. New York: Princeton Architectural Press, 2010.

McCarthy, Jane, and Laurily Keir Epstein. *A Guide to the Sculpture Parks and Gardens of America*. New York: Kesend, 1996.

Mozingo, Louise A. *Pastoral Capitalism: A History of Suburban Corporate Landscapes*. Cambridge, MA: MIT Press, 2011.

Nicolin, Pierluigi, and Francesco Repishti. *Dictionary of Today's Landscape Designers*. Milan: Skira, 2003.

Treib, Marc. *Modern Landscape Architecture: A Critical Review*. Cambridge, MA: MIT Press, 1994.

Uffelen, Chris van. *Art in Public: 500 Masterpieces From the Ancient World to the Present*. Salentstein, Switzerland: Braun, 2011.

Weilacher, Udo. *Between Landscape Architecture and Land Art*. Basel: Birkäuser, 1995.

INDEX

CREDITS

2, 69: Cao | Perrot Studio, *Lullaby Garden*. Photograph by Stephen Jerrome. *Vietnamese Lullaby*: Huong Thanh & Nguyen Le. Courtesy of the Cornerstone Gardens and Cao | Perrot Studio.

6, 96: John Ruppert, *Orb*, 2009, Baltimore Museum of Art. Medium: Anodized aluminum chain-link fabric and stainless steel. 14 × 16 ft. (diameter). Courtesy of Baltimore Museum of Art and John Ruppert.

12, 50: Type A (American, founded 1998), *Team Building (Align)*, 2010. Indianapolis Museum of Art.

14, 17, 105: Christine Tarkowski, *Working on the Failed Utopia*, 2005. Courtesy of Christine Tarkowski, Nathan Manilow Sculpture Park. © Photograph by Michelle Litvin.

18, 68: Topher Delaney, *Garden Play*, 2009. Courtesy of the Cornerstone Gardens and Topher Delaney.

20 top: Margaret Evangeline, *Gunshot Landscape*, 2004. Courtesy of The Fields Sculpture Park at Omi International Arts Center and Margaret Evangeline.

20 bottom: Oliver Kruse, *Clench*, 2008. Courtesy of The Fields Sculpture Park at Omi International Arts Center and Oliver Kruse.

21: Roy Staab, *Green Galleon*, 2008. Courtesy of The Fields Sculpture Park at Omi International Arts Center and Roy Staab.

22–23: Charles Ginnever, *Apollo*, 1985. Courtesy of The Fields Sculpture Park at Omi International Arts Center and Charles Ginnever.

24–25: Bernar Venet, *5 Arcs × 5*, 2000. Cor-Ten steel, 410 × 415 × 90 cm. each. Courtesy of The Fields Sculpture Park at Omi International Arts Center and Bernar Venet.

26: Larry W. Griffis Jr., *Rohr Hill Sculptures*. Courtesy of Griffis Sculpture Park. © Photograph by Piotr Rotkiewicz.

27: Frank Fantauzzi, Mehrdad Hadighi, *Wood Pallet Egg*, 2010. Courtesy of Frank Fantauzzi, Mehrdad Hadighi, Griffis Sculpture Park. © Photograph by Piotr Rotkiewicz.

28 top: Steven Siegel, *Facing Love; 30*, 1999. Courtesy of Stone Quarry Hill Art Park and Steven Siegel.

28 bottom: John von Bergen, *Grande Comore II*, 2004. Courtesy of Stone Quarry Hill Art Park and John von Bergen.

29: Sook Jin Jo, *Meditation Space*, 2000. Courtesy of Stone Quarry Hill Art Park and Sook Jin Jo.

30: Maya Lin, *Storm King Wave Field*, 2009. Courtesy of Storm King Art Center and Maya Lin. Photograph by Jerry L. Thompson.

32–33: Mark di Suvero (1933–). View of the South Fields, Mark di Suvero sculptures. Left to right: *Pyramidian*, 1987/98. Steel, 65 ft. × 46 ft. × 46 ft. *Mon Père, Mon Père*, 1973–75. Steel, 35 ft. × 40 ft. × 40 ft. 4 in.; *Mother Peace*, 1969–70. Painted steel, 41 ft. 8 in. × 49 ft. 5 in. × 44 ft. 3 in. Gift of the Ralph E. Ogden Foundation, Inc. Photograph by Jerry L. Thompson. © Storm King Art Center, Mountainville, New York.

34: Alissa Neglia, (from the exhibition, Escape Velocity) *Lace*, 1998. Steel, wood 16 × 32 × 2 ft. Courtesy of Socrates Sculpture Park. Photograph by Steven L. Cohen.

35: Lishan Chang, *LC Space @ SSP*, 2007 (from the exhibition *Float*, 2007). Plastic stretch wrap, wooden poles, trees. Dimensions variable. Courtesy of Socrates Sculpture Park.

36 top: Isaac Witkin, *Eolith*, 1994. Courtesy of The Sculpture Foundation, Inc. Sited at Grounds For Sculpture, Hamilton, NJ. Photograph by David Steele.

36 bottom: Carlos Dorrien, *The Nine Muses*, 1990–97. Courtesy of The Sculpture Foundation, Inc. Sited at Grounds For Sculpture, Hamilton, NJ. Photograph by David Steele.

38–39: Steven Siegel, *Grass, Paper, Glass*, 2006. Courtesy of The Sculpture Foundation, Inc. Sited at Grounds For Sculpture, Hamilton, NJ.

40 top: Nils-Udo, *Clemson Clay Nest*, 2005. Clay, pinetrees, bamboos. Botanical Garden of South Carolina, Clemson, USA. Lifochrome on dibond 87 × 100 cm. ed.8. Courtesy of Nils-Udo.

40 bottom: Herb Parker, *Crucible*, 1995. Courtesy of the South Carolina Botanical Garden.

41: Brian Rust, *Earthen Bridge*, 1996. Courtesy of the South Carolina Botanical Garden.

42: Lin Emery, *Duo*, 1992. Courtesy of the Museum of Outdoor Arts.

43: Patrick Dougherty, *Stickwork*, 2008. Courtesy of Kara Primomo for the Museum of Outdoor Arts.

44–45: Sanfte Strukturen-Marcel Kalberer, *Weidenblume*, 2010. Courtesy of Sanfte Strukturen-Marcel Kalberer, Anna Kalberer, Dorothea Kalberer, Peedy Evacic, Bernadette Mercx.

46: Kenneth Snelson, *B-Tree II*, 2005. Stainless steel, h. 384 in. Frederik Meijer Gardens & Sculpture Park, Grand Rapids, Michigan. Gift of Fred and Lena Meijer. Courtesy of Kenneth Snelson.

47: Andy Goldsworthy, *Grand Rapids Arch*, 2001–5. Stone, h. 216 in. Frederik Meijer Gardens & Sculpture Park, Grand Rapids, Michigan. Gift of Fred and Lena Meijer. Courtesy of Galerie Lelong, New York.

48–49: Magdalena Abakanowicz, *Figure on a Trunk*, 1998. Bronze, h. 96 in. Frederik Meijer Gardens & Sculpture Park, Grand Rapids, Michigan. Gift of Fred and Lena Meijer. Courtesy of Marlborough Gallery, New York.

51: Andrea Zittel (American, 1965–), *Indy Island*, 2010. Indianapolis Museum of Art.

52–53: Jeppe Hein (Danish, 1974–), *Bench Around the Lake*, 2010. Indianapolis Museum of Art.

54: Thomas Sternal, *Cage Form*, 1990. Courtesy of Cedarhurst Center for the Arts.

55: Martha Enzmann, *Dancers*, 1993–94. Courtesy of Cedarhurst Center for the Arts.

56–57: Andy Zimmermann, *Crossroads*, 1994. Courtesy of Cedarhurst Center for the Arts.

58 top: Millennium Park, Courtesy of the Commissioner of the Department of Cultural Affairs–Millennium Park, Chicago. © Photograph by Peter Schulz.

58 bottom: Spencer Finch, *Lunar*, 2011. Two solar panels with charger, light-emitting diodes, lamp fixture, lead, aluminum, stainless steel and polycarbonate. Courtesy of Spencer Finch and Rhona Hoffman Gallery, Chicago.

60 top: Donald Lipski (1947–), *Ball? Ball! Wall? Wall!*, 1994. 55 steel marine buoys. Laumeier Sculpture Park Collection. Gift of Terri Hyland. Photograph by Mike Venso/Laumeier Sculpture Park.

60 bottom: Mary Miss (1944–), *Pool Complex: Orchard Valley*, 1983–85. Wolmanized pine, concrete, stone, galvanized ferrous metal. Laumeier Sculpture Park Commission. Photograph by Mike Venso/Laumeier Sculpture Park.

62–63: Vito Acconci (1940–), *Face of the Earth #3*, 1988. Natural concrete, gravel, reinforced rods, sod and earth. Laumeier Sculpture Park Commission. Gift of Vito Acconci. Photograph by Mike Venso/Laumeier Sculpture Park.

64–65: Jene Highstein (1942–), *Ada's Will*, 1990. Steel-reinforced and painted concrete. Laumeier Sculpture Park Commission. Photograph by Mike Venso/Laumeier Sculpture Park.

66: Isamu Noguchi, *California Scenario*, 1980–82. © Photograph by Steve Aldana.

67: Isamu Noguchi, *California Scenario*, 1980–82. © Photograph by Wayne Daniels.

70: Claude Cormier, *Blue Tree*, 2004. Courtesy of Claude Cormier + Associés Inc. Photograph courtesy the Cornerstone Gardens.

71: Yoji Sasaki, *The Garden of Visceral Serenity*. Courtesy of the Cornerstone Gardens and Yoji Sasaki.

72–75: Weiss/Manfredi Architects, *Olympic Sculpture Park*. © Photograph by Benjamin Benschneider. Courtesy of Weiss/Manfredi Architects.

76, 89: Raphael Zollinger, *Welcome*, 2005. © Photograph by Bob Handelman. Courtesy of the Pratt Institute.

78: Yoshio Taniguchi (1937–): Abby Aldrich Rockefeller Sculpture Garden, Museum of Modern Art, 2004. New York, Museum of Modern Art (MoMA). Photograph by Timothy Hursley. 84066. © 2012. Digital Image, Timothy Hursley/The Museum of Modern Art, New York/Scala, Firenze.

80–81: Yoshio Taniguchi (1937–): Abby Aldrich Rockefeller Sculpture Garden, Museum of Modern Art, 2004. New York, Museum of Modern Art (MoMA). Photograph by Timothy Hursley. 82047. © 2012. Digital Image, Timothy Hursley/The Museum of Modern Art, New York/Scala, Firenze.

82: Mike and Doug Starn, *Big Bambú: You Can't, You Don't, and You Won't Stop*. The Metropolitan Museum of Art, NYC, 2010. Courtesy of Mike and Doug Starn, 2012.

84–85: Roxy Paine, *Maelstrom*, 2009. Stainless steel. The Metropolitan Museum of Art, NYC, 2009. Courtesy of Roxy Paine.

86 top: Ball-Nogues, *Liquid Sky*, 2007. Courtesy of Ball-Nogues. © Photograph by Mark Lentz. Courtesy of PS1 Contemporary Art Center.

86 bottom: Ball-Nogues, *Liquid Sky*, 2007. Courtesy of Ball-Nogues. © Photograph by Steph Goralnick. Courtesy of PS1 Contemporary Art Center.

88: Pratt Institute Sculpture Garden. © Photograph by Pratt Institute.

90: Richard Serra, *Stacks*, 1990. Photograph by Francesca Cigola.

92: Louise Nevelson, *Transparent Horizon*, 1975. Welded Cor-Ten steel, painted, 240 × 252 × 97 in. © Photograph by Roxanne Everett. Copyright Lippincott LLC.

94: Henry Moore (British, 1898–1986), *Oval with Points*. Bronze, h. 335.0 cm. Courtesy of The John B. Putnam Jr. Memorial Collection, Princeton University, 1969–70. © Photograph by Bruce M. White. Reproduced by permission of The Henry Moore Foundation.

98: View of the Sculpture Garden and Plaza. Hirshhorn Museum and Sculpture Garden, Smithsonian Institution. Photograph by Lee Stalsworth.

100: Hector Guimard, *An Entrance to the Paris Metropolitan*, 1902–13. Photograph by Francesca Cigola.

102–3: Melvin Charney, *Esplanade Ernest Cormier*, 1989. Photograph by Francesca Cigola.

104 top: Mark di Suvero, *Yes! For Lady Day*, 1968–69. © Photograph by Geoffrey Bates, Nathan Manilow Sculpture Park, Governors State University.

104 bottom: Mary Miss, *Field Rotation*, 1981. Courtesy of Mary Miss, Nathan Manilow Sculpture Park, Governors State University.

106: Minneapolis Sculpture Garden. Courtesy of Walker Art Center.

108: Jaume Plensa (Spanish, 1955–), *Nomade*, 2007. Painted stainless steel, 324 × 204 in. Promised gift from John and Mary Pappajohn to the Des Moines Art Center. Courtesy of Des Moines Art Center and Jaume Plensa. © Photograph by Cameron Campbell.

109: John and Mary Pappajohn Sculpture Park, view from the east. Courtesy of Des Moines Art Center. © Photograph by Cameron Campbell.

110–11: Louise Bourgeois (American, born France 1911–died United States 2010), *Spider*, 1997. Bronze, 90 × 88 × 86 in. Promised gift from John and Mary Pappajohn to the Des Moines Art Center. © Photograph courtesy of Connie Wilson.

112 top: Kansas City Sculpture Park, Nelson-Atkins Museum of Art. Courtesy of Steven Holl Architects. © Photograph by Andy Ryan.

112 bottom: Claes Oldenburg and Coosje van Bruggen, *Shuttlecocks*, 1994. Aluminum and fiber-reinforced plastic; painted with polyurethane enamel. Four shuttlecocks, each 17 ft. 11 in. (5. 5 m) high × 15 ft. 1 in. (4.6 m) crown diameter and 4 ft. (1.2 m) nose cone diameter, sited in different positions on the grounds of the museum. Collection of The Nelson-Atkins Museum of Art, Kansas City.

114–15: Tony Cragg, *Turbo*, 2001. Courtesy of Steven Holl Architects. © Photograph by Andy Ryan.

116: Serge Yourievitch (French 1876–1969), *La Danseuse Nattova*, 1925. Bronze Gift of Mrs. Bessie Mussey, Courtesy of Birmingham Museum of Art.

117: Charles W. Ireland Sculpture Park, Birmingham Museum of Art. Courtesy of Birmingham Museum of Art.

118: George Segal (1924–2000), *Couple on Two Benches*, 1985; cast 1989. Bronze with white patina and metal benches, 3/5. Hunter Museum of American Art, Chattanooga, Tennessee, Museum purchase with funds from the Hunter Museum of Art Acquisition Foundation, 1989.9.

119: Hunter Museum Sculpture Plaza. Courtesy of Hunter Museum of American Art.

120: Steve Tobin (American, 1957–), *Steel Roots*, 2008. Painted steel, 180 × 240 × 192 in. The Frost Art Museum. Courtesy of Steve Tobin. FIU L2008.3.2. © Photography by Ken Ek.

121: Steve Tobin (American, 1957–), *Steel Roots*, 2002. Cast bronze & painted patina 216 × 108 × 72 in. The Frost Art Museum. Courtesy of Steve Tobin. FIU L2003.20. © Photography by Ken Ek.

122–23: Mark Di Suvero, *Ave*, 1973. Painted steel. Overall: 478 × 370 × 545 in. (12 m 14.12 cm × 9 m 39.8 cm × 13 m 84.3 cm). Weight: 12000 lb. (5443.1643 kg). Dallas Museum of Art, Irvin L. and Meryl P. Levy Endowment Fund. © Photograph by Dallas Museum of Art.

124–25: Dallas Museum of Art Sculpture Garden. © Photograph by Dallas Museum of Art.

126, 130–31: Nasher Sculpture Garden. Photograph courtesy of Peter Walker and Partners. © Photograph by Tim Hursley. Reproduced with the permission of the Nasher Sculpture Center, Dallas.

128–29: Nasher Sculpture Garden. Photograph courtesy of Peter Walker and Partners. Reproduced with the permission of the Nasher Sculpture Center, Dallas. Photograph by Peter Walker.

132: Detailed view of the Cullen Sculpture Garden, RG36-1097-001, 2005. Photograph by Rocky Kneten, Museum of Fine Arts, Houston, Archives.

134–35: North view into the Cullen Sculpture Garden, RG36-395-003 a, 8/1990. Photograph by Tom DuBrock. Museum of Fine Arts, Houston, Archives.

136 top: The Menil Collection, 1982–87, Houston, Texas, USA. © Piano & Fitzgerald, architects. Courtesy of RPBW.

136 bottom: Michael Heizer (1944–), *Isolated Mass/Circumflex (#2)*, 1968–72. Mayari-R steel, 12 in. × 8 ft. 8 in. × 115 ft (30.5 × 259.2 × 3,505.2 cm). Photograph by Hickey-Robertson, Houston. © Michael Heizer, 2011. The Menil Collection, Houston.

138 top: John Roloff, *Fragment: the Hidden Sea (Island of Refuge)*, 1993. Collection of Stanford University. © Photograph by John Roloff.

138 bottom: Bruce Beasley, *Vanguard*, 1980 burnished stainless steel, 28' wide. Collection of Stanford University. © Photograph by Bruce Beasley.

140: Auguste Rodin (French, 1840–1917), *The Walking Man*, 1905. Bronze; 83¾ × 35 × 17 inches (213 × 88.9 × 43.2 cm) Foundry: Georges Rudier, Paris. Gift of the UCLA Alumni Association and an anonymous donor as a tribute to Franklin D. Murphy, 1967. Photograph by Joshua White. Courtesy of the Hammer Museum, Los Angeles.

142–43: Franklin D. Murphy Sculpture Garden with Gerhard Marcks's *Maja*, 1941. Bronze; 88 × 25 × 23 inches (223.5 × 63.5 × 58.4 cm) Foundry: H. Noack, Berlin. Gift of Mr. and Mrs. Jack Warner and the UCLA Art Council, 1970. Photograph by Joshua White, Courtesy of the Hammer Museum, Los Angeles. © Gerhard-Marcks-Stiftung, Bremen 2012.

144: Chris Burden, *Urban Light*, 2008. Courtesy of Gagosian Gallery. Photograph by Museum Associates LACMA 2012.

146–47: Alexander Calder (United States, Pennsylvania, Philadelphia, 1898–1976), *Three Quintains*, 1964. Sculpture, Painted metal, mobile, Overall: 275 × 288 inches (698.5 × 731.52 cm). Art Museum Council Fund (M.65.10). © Photograph by Museum Associates/LACMA 2012.

148: Giacomo Manzù, *Cardinale seduto*, 1975–77. Courtesy of The J. Paul Getty Museum, Los Angeles, Gift of Fran and Ray Stark.

150 top: Gustav Kraitz (Swedish, b. 1926), *Apple*, 2005. Glazed ceramic, 44.5 × 41.9 × 41.9 cm (17½ × 16½ × 16½ in.). Fine Arts Museums of San Francisco, Gift of Barbro and Bernard A. Osher to the Fine Arts, 2005. 94.1.

150 bottom: Juan Muñoz (Spanish, 1953–2001), *Conversation Piece V*, 2001. Bronze, 64 × 31⅜ × 31⅜ in. (162.6 × 79.7 × 79.7 cm); 64 × 31⅜ × 31⅜ in. (162.6 × 79.7 × 79.7 cm); 64 × 31⅜ × 31⅜ in. (162.6 × 79.7 × 79.7 cm). Fine Arts Museums of San Francisco, Foundation Purchase, Gift of Barbro and Bernard A. Osher, 2005.125a-c.

151: View of the Museum Building. Courtesy of Fine Arts Museums of San Francisco.

152–53: Claes Oldenburg (American, 1929–) and Coosje van Bruggen (American, 1942–2009), *Corridor Pin, Blue*, 1999. Stainless steel and aluminum, painted with polyurethane enamel, 647.7 × 645.2 × 40.6 cm (255 × 254 × 16 in.). Fine Arts Museums, gift of the Barbro Osher Pro Suecia Foundation, 2003.66a-b. Henry Moore (English, 1898–1986), *Bildgiesserei Hermann Noack* (maker, German, b. 1897), *Two Piece Reclining Figure No. 9*, 1968. Cast bronze, 143.2 × 243.8 × 132.1 cm (56⅜ × 96 × 52 in.). Gift of George Quist and Robin Quist Gates, 2001.194. Barbara Hepworth (English, 1902–75), *Pierced Monolith with Colour*, 1965. Roman stone and paint, 68½ × 46 × 8 in. Foundation purchase, gift of Barbro and Bernard A. Osher, 2003.110. James Turrell (American, 1943–), *Three Gems*, 2005. Concrete, plaster, stone and neon lighting. Foundation purchase, gift of Barbro and Bernard A. Osher, 2003.68.

Published by:
Princeton Architectural Press
37 East 7th Street
New York, New York 10003

Visit our website at www.papress.com

First published in Italy in 2013 by Sassi Editore srl
© 2013 Sassi Editore srl
Text © 2013 Francesca Cigola
English translation © 2013 Princeton Architectural Press

For Sassi Editore srl:
Editor: Luca Sassi
Copy editor: Francesca Marotto
Designer: Matteo Gaule
Color separations: Sassi editore srl

For Princeton Architectural Press:
Translator: Natalie Danford
Editor: Sara E. Stemen
Typesetting: Benjamin English

Special thanks to:
Meredith Baber, Sara Bader, Nicola Bednarek Brower, Janet Behning,
Fannie Bushin, Megan Carey, Carina Cha, Andrea Chlad,
Russell Fernandez, Emily Johnston-O'Neill, Jan Hartman, Jan Haux,
Jennifer Lippert, Diane Levinson, Katharine Myers, Margaret Rogalski,
Dan Simon, Andrew Stepanian, Elana Schlenker, Paul Wagner,
and Joseph Weston of Princeton Architectural Press
—Kevin C. Lippert, publisher

Library of Congress Cataloging-in-Publication Data

Cigola, Francesca.
  [Artscapes. English]
  Art parks : a tour of America's sculpture parks and gardens /
Francesca Cigola. – First [edition].
      pages cm
  ISBN 978-1-61689-129-9 (hardback)
  1. Sculpture parks–United States–Guidebooks.
  2. Sculpture gardens–United States–Guidebooks. I. Title.
  NB1278.C5413 2013
  730.74'73–dc23
                                2012041006